LEARN SPANISH WITH PICTURES

LEARN SPANISH WITH PICTURES

The Easy, Visual Way to Master Basic Grammar and Vocabulary

Melanie Stuart-Campbell

Illustrations by Dalton Webb

ROCKRIDGE
PRESS

**To my South American street dog,
for inspiring me to create Alba's Spanish Tales.**

Copyright © 2019 Rockridge Press, Emeryville, California

No part of this publication may be reproduced, stored in a retrieval system, or transmitted in any form or by any means, electronic, mechanical, photocopying, recording, scanning, or otherwise, except as permitted under Sections 107 or 108 of the 1976 United States Copyright Act, without the prior written permission of the Publisher. Requests to the Publisher for permission should be addressed to the Permissions Department, Rockridge Press, 6005 Shellmound Street, Suite 175, Emeryville, CA 94608.

Limit of Liability/Disclaimer of Warranty: The Publisher and the author make no representations or warranties with respect to the accuracy or completeness of the contents of this work and specifically disclaim all warranties, including without limitation warranties of fitness for a particular purpose. No warranty may be created or extended by sales or promotional materials. The advice and strategies contained herein may not be suitable for every situation. This work is sold with the understanding that the Publisher is not engaged in rendering medical, legal, or other professional advice or services. If professional assistance is required, the services of a competent professional person should be sought. Neither the Publisher nor the author shall be liable for damages arising herefrom. The fact that an individual, organization, or website is referred to in this work as a citation and/or potential source of further information does not mean that the author or the Publisher endorses the information the individual, organization, or website may provide or recommendations they/it may make. Further, readers should be aware that websites listed in this work may have changed or disappeared between when this work was written and when it is read.

For general information on our other products and services or to obtain technical support, please contact our Customer Care Department within the United States at (866) 744-2665, or outside the United States at (510) 253-0500.

Rockridge Press publishes its books in a variety of electronic and print formats. Some content that appears in print may not be available in electronic books, and vice versa.

TRADEMARKS: Rockridge Press and the Rockridge Press logo are trademarks or registered trademarks of Callisto Media Inc. and/or its affiliates, in the United States and other countries, and may not be used without written permission. All other trademarks are the property of their respective owners. Rockridge Press is not associated with any product or vendor mentioned in this book.

Interior and Cover Designer: Emma Hall
Art Producer: Sue Bischofberger
Editor: Marisa A. Hines
Production Manager: Oriana Siska
Production Editor: Melissa Edeburn

Illustrations © 2019 Dalton Webb

ISBN: Print 978-1-64152-408-7 | eBook 978-1-64152-409-4

R0

CONTENTS

INTRODUCTION

When I first speak Spanish to someone, I sometimes am asked, *¿De dónde es usted?* ("Where are you from?") Some people are surprised to learn that I'm a fourth-generation Kansan with primarily Anglo ancestry. They sometimes ask why I speak Spanish. This question allows me to share with them how I value their language. After they have heard my reasons, I am able to establish a positive intention. I hope to validate their language and culture and, by extension, that person as an individual. Nelson Mandela had it right when he said, "If you talk to a man in a language he understands, that goes to his head. If you talk to him in his own language, that goes to his heart."

My own journey through the beautiful Spanish language started in a university class and continues to this day. My Spanish proficiency is a combination of formal coursework, study and travel abroad, teaching overseas, reading and listening to music in Spanish, and—most importantly—just talking to people who speak and understand *español*.

There are several reasons to study and develop some basic language skills in Spanish. And it's never too late to start learning! Up until I attended the University of Kansas, the only Spanish I knew was how to count to ten. Not only is Spanish the second-most spoken language in the United States, it is also the dominant language in many countries. Globally, Spanish is used by approximately 435 million people, and it is the second-most spoken language worldwide. So, the ability to communicate in Spanish opens up large parts of the world to you!

I love learning and teaching languages. I received my undergraduate degree in secondary education, with a Spanish major and a French minor. My graduate degree is in applied linguistics, and my teaching jobs over the years—in Kansas, New York, Ecuador, and the Republic of Congo—have all been related to acquiring other languages and improving the lives of language learners. Today, I use Spanish on a daily basis in my position at an educational service center. Without my Spanish skills, I would not be effective in communicating with the many families and students I'm honored to serve.

When you complete all the lessons and quizzes (and practice *mucho*), you should be able to confidently navigate your way through the real-life situations that are presented in this book. You will avoid overpaying or getting lost and will be able to communicate with a doctor or a police officer while in a Spanish-speaking country or neighborhood. Those are just a few benefits of studying this book!

You will also appreciate the easy-to-follow format of the lessons while getting to know your illustrated "language guides": Mateo, María, Paco, Stuart, and Paloma! The proverb "a picture is worth a thousand words" is true, and the illustrations in this book will greatly assist you with the most important words and phrases in a manageable and fun way. Have a great time on your language adventure when you *Learn Spanish with Pictures*!

HOW TO USE THIS BOOK

This book is divided into 101 lessons that feature *Key Terms and Phrases* that pertain to the lesson's topic. The *Conversation* section then shows you how to use those *Key Terms and Phrases* correctly when speaking.

Each lesson features an illustration representing the specific topic and includes "Spanish language guides" who speak with each other about that particular topic. These language guides, three adults and two children whom you see throughout the book, are in situations where you as a Spanish learner may find yourself one day.

The lessons involve real-life circumstances that integrate cultural, historical, and geographical content that will enhance your overall competence in "all things Spanish." Moreover, the lessons are divided into themes that relate to each other. For example, the category "Getting to Know You" includes the lessons "Do You Speak Spanish?," "Where Are You From?," and "How's the Family?," just to name a few.

To test your knowledge of the newly introduced *Key Terms and Phrases* and how they are used in conversation, you'll find *Questions* and *Answers* sections at the end of each lesson. You will also have the opportunity to assess your understanding with the 25 *Quizzes* that are included throughout the book.

Some lessons also feature a *Remember* and/or *Notes* component. Under *Remember* you will be reminded of an important Spanish language detail that will assist you in your comprehension of the lesson you are studying. Under *Notes* you will find additional information that may (1) provide more context about the lesson, (2) offer regional variations, (3) present alternative terms and phrases, or (4) include cultural expectations and norms.

The 101 lessons increase in complexity, and you must apply what you are studying to truly learn it. In other words, practice speaking a lot, and rest assured that one day you can be proficient in Spanish!

PRONUNCIATION GUIDE

Spanish words are generally pronounced phonetically, or the way they are written. Spanish has the same alphabet as English with four additional letters: *ch, ll, ñ,* and *rr*.

Below is the Spanish alphabet and its pronunciation. The [brackets] indicate how to pronounce the name of the letter. It is important to note that the names of Spanish letters have one, two, and in a couple cases, three or four syllables. The syllable to stress (pronounce more loudly) is the syllable written in ALL CAPS.

The Vowels

- *a* [ah]: as the *a* in **far**
- *e* [eh]: as the *e* in **best**
- *i* [ee]: as the *i* in **routine**
- *o* [oh]: as the *o* in **over**
- *u* [oo]: as the *oo* in **pool**

> *Note: The letter *i* in Spanish is pronounced just like the letter *e* in English, which can be confusing at times.

The Consonants Most Different from English

- *c* [seh]: as the *k* in **kite** when it is before *a, o,* and *u* (as in **casa**, **cosa**, and **culpa**), and as the *s* in **sad** when it is before *e* or *i* (as in **cena** and **cita**)
- *ch* [cheh]: as the *ch* in **child**
- *g* [geh]: as the *h* in **hello**
- *h* [AH-cheh]: as the *h* in **honest** (it is silent)
- *j* [HOH-tah]: as the *h* in **hot**
- *ll* [EH-yeh]: as the *y* in **you**
- *ñ* [EH-nyeh]: as the *ny* in **canyon**
- *rr* [EH-rreh]: this is a sound English does not have, the rolled or trilled *r*
- *z* [SEH-tah]: as the *s* in **sun** (a Spanish example is the name **Zara**, in which the *z* is pronounced like the *s* in the English name **Sara**)

The Consonants Most Similar to English

- *b* [beh]: often called the "b de burro"
- *d* [deh]: to pronounce *d* in Spanish, place the tip of your tongue behind your front teeth and not on the roof of your mouth (as in English)
- *f* [EH-feh]
- *k* [kah]
- *l* [EH-leh]
- *m* [EH-meh]
- *n* [EH-neh]
- *p* [peh]
- *q* [koo]
- *r* [EH-reh]
- *s* [EH-seh]
- *t* [teh]
- *v* [veh]: in Latin America, *v* is pronunced like *b* as in **boy**; often called the "v de vaca"
- *w* [DOH-bleh-veh]
- *x* [EH-kees]
- *y* [ee-gree-EH-gah]

101 Lessons and Quizzes

Greetings

It's Nice to Meet You

Key Terms and Phrases

Buenos días	Good morning
Me llamo	My name is
¿Cómo se llama?	What is your name? (formal)
usted	you (formal)
Mucho gusto	Nice to meet you

Conversation

MATEO   Buenos días, me llamo Mateo. Mucho gusto. ¿Cómo se llama usted?

> **NOTES**
> Because Mateo and the gentleman are meeting for the first time, they are using the formal form of the word *you* in Spanish, which is *usted*.

Questions

1. What is the man's name? *Mateo*
2. How does he say *Good morning* to the other man? **Buenos días**
3. How does he say *Nice to meet you?* **Mucho gusto**
4. How does he say *What is your name?* **¿Como se llama usted?**

Answers: 1. Mateo   **2.** Buenos días   **3.** Mucho gusto   **4.** ¿Cómo se llama usted?

It's Nice to Meet You, Too

Key Terms and Phrases

Igualmente	Same to you
y tú	and you (informal)
¿Cómo te llamas?	What is your (informal) name?
Paloma es mi vecina.	Paloma is my neighbor.
también	too
los niños	children
señor/a	sir/ma'am (Mr./Ms.)
Soy amigo de . . .	I'm a friend of . . .

Conversation

JUAN Igualmente, Mateo. Me llamo Juan. ¿Y tú? ¿Cómo te llamas?

PALOMA Buenos días. Me llamo Paloma.

MATEO Paloma es mi vecina.

JUAN ¿Y tú? ¿Cómo te llamas?

STUART Me llamo Stuart. Mucho gusto.

MATEO Stuart es mi vecino también.

JUAN Mucho gusto, niños.

JUAN ¿Y usted, señor, cómo se llama?

PACO Me llamo Paco. Soy amigo de Mateo, Stuart y Paloma.

> **REMEMBER**
> *Usted* is the formal term for *you* used by people who have just met.

NOTES

Igualmente is an abbreviated way to say *Nice to meet you, too*.

Vos is used instead of *tú* in some parts of Central America and also throughout Uruguay and Argentina.

Because Juan is talking to a child, even if they're meeting for the first time, he is using the informal form of the word *you* in Spanish, which is *tú*.

Buenos días literally means *Good day* but is used to greet people until approximately noon.

Questions

1. What is the other man's name? Juan

2. How does he say *Nice to meet you, too*? mucho gusto

3. How does he ask the girl her name? ¿Como te llanas?

4. What is the girl's name? Paloma

5. What is the boy's name? Stuart

6. What's the name of the man who is friends with Mateo, Stuart, and Paloma? Paco.

Answers: 1. Juan   2. Igualmente   3. ¿Cómo te llamas?   4. Paloma   5. Stuart   6. Paco

Please Spell Your Name

Key Terms and Phrases

el nombre	name
su	your (formal)
y	and
tu	your (informal)
Gracias	Thank you
se escribe	it is written

Conversation

MATEO ¿Cómo se escribe su nombre, Juan?

JUAN J-U-A-N

MATEO Gracias.

NOTES
Even though *se escribe* is literally translated as "it is written," it's used in situations to spell words.

Questions

1. What does *nombre* mean in English? name

2. How does Juan spell his name in Spanish? Juan

3. How does Mateo ask Juan how he spells his name? Como se escribe su nombre

4. What does *Gracias* mean in English? thank you

Answers: 1. name   2. J-U-A-N   3. ¿Cómo se escribe su nombre?   4. Thank you.

Let Me Introduce You

Key Terms and Phrases

Hola	Hello
Te presento a mis nuevos amigos.	I introduce you (informal) to my new friends.
el amigo	friend (male)
Juan es mi esposo.	Juan is my husband.

Conversation

JUAN   Hola, Silvia.

SILVIA   Hola, Juan.

JUAN   Silvia, te presento a mis nuevos amigos. Son Mateo y María.

SILVIA   Mucho gusto. Juan es mi esposo.

JUAN   Les presento a Silvia.

REMEMBER

Usted is used for people when they first meet (and until more familiarity develops in the relationship). It is also used by anyone younger when speaking to someone older (child to an older person).

NOTES

Juan used the informal *te presento* when introducing Silvia to everyone because she is his wife. *Tú* is used between people already familiar with each other and for children (regardless of the duration of the relationship). Juan then used *les presento* when introducing more than one person to his wife. If he had introduced only one person (whom he'd just met) to his wife, he'd have said *le presento* instead of *les presento*.

Questions

1. How do you know Juan and Silvia are already familiar with each other?

2. Why does Juan use *les presento* when introducing his two new park acquaintances to his wife?

Answers: 1. Because Juan says *te presento* when introducing his wife to his new park acquaintances. *Te* signifies a familiar relationship.   2. Because he's introducing more than one person to his wife.

Let Me Introduce You: Children

Key Terms and Phrases

Buenas tardes	Good afternoon

Conversation

PALOMA Buenas tardes, me llamo Paloma.

DIEGO Buenas tardes, me llamo Diego.

PALOMA Stuart, te presento a Diego.

STUART Mucho gusto, Diego.

DIEGO Igualmente.

> **NOTES**
> *Buenas tardes* is used between noon and evening time.

Questions

1. How do you say *Good afternoon* in Spanish?

2. Why does Paloma use *te presento* when speaking to Stuart?

3. How does Stuart say *Nice to meet you* to Diego?

Answers: 1. Buenas tardes   2. Because they're children.   3. Mucho gusto

Lessons 1–5

Match the English word or phrase with its Spanish translation.

Spanish words and phrases				
Hola	Igualmente	¿Cómo se escribe?	¿Cómo se llama?	amigo
Buenos días	Señora	Te presento	Gracias	Señor
nombre	Mucho gusto	Me llamo		

1. Thank you _____

2. How do you spell that? _____

3. Hello _____

4. name _____

5. What is your (formal) name? _____

6. Nice to meet you _____

7. Same (to you) _____

8. Good morning _____

9. My name is _____

10. I present to you (for introducing people) _____

11. friend _____

12. Ms. or Mrs. _____

13. Mr. _____

Getting to
Know You

Do You Speak Spanish?

Key Terms and Phrases

¿Habla español?	Do you (singular, formal) speak Spanish?
¿Hablan español?	Do you (plural) speak Spanish?
un poco	a little
Sí, mucho.	Yes, a lot.
No hablo mucho español.	I don't speak much Spanish.
el inglés	English
ustedes	you (plural)
¿Cómo se dice?	How do you say?
Se dice "Estoy aprendiendo".	You say, "I'm learning."

Conversation

JUAN ¿Hablan español ustedes?

STUART No hablo mucho español, sólo un poco. Hablo inglés.

PALOMA Sí, hablo mucho. ¿Y tú, Diego, hablas mucho español?

DIEGO Sí.

STUART ¿Cómo se dice "I'm learning" en español?

PALOMA Se dice "Estoy aprendiendo".

STUART ¿Y usted, señor, habla español?

JUAN Sí.

CONTINUED

REMEMBER

Tú is almost always used when speaking to a child and between children. Children must use *Usted* with adults; using *tú* is considered disrespectful.

NOTES

To make a sentence negative, as in *I don't speak Spanish*, simply put the word *no* in front of the verb, as in *No hablo*.

In Spanish you do not capitalize the language name. For example, *Spanish* is written with an uppercase letter in English, but *español* is written with a lowercase letter in Spanish. Unless the name of the language is the first word in a sentence, do not capitalize it.

Questions

1. How much Spanish does Stuart speak?

2. Does Paloma speak Spanish?

3. How does Paloma ask Diego if he speaks Spanish?

4. How does Juan ask the children if they speak Spanish?

5. How does Stuart ask Juan if he speaks Spanish?

6. How do you say *How do you say?* in Spanish?

Answers: 1. a little **2.** Yes. **3.** ¿Y tú, Diego, hablas mucho español? **4.** ¿Hablan español ustedes? **5.** ¿Y usted, señor, habla español? **6.** ¿Cómo se dice?

Where Are You From?

> **REMEMBER**
> The subject pronoun (*I, you* (singular), *he,
> she, it, we, you* (plural), and *they*) is usually
> not used before the verb in Spanish.

Key Terms and Phrases

¿De dónde son ustedes?	Where are you (plural) from?
¿De dónde eres?	Where are you (singular informal) from?
¿De dónde es?	Where are you (singular formal) from? or Where is he/she from?
Es de los Estados Unidos.	He/she is from the United States.
Soy de . . .	I'm from . . .

Conversation

MATEO Soy de Paraguay. ¿De dónde son ustedes?

PACO Soy de Puerto Rico. Stuart es de los Estados Unidos.

MATEO ¿De dónde eres, Paloma?

PALOMA Soy de Costa Rica.

MATEO ¿De dónde eres, María?

MARÍA Soy de Chile.

Questions

1. Where is Stuart from?
2. Which two people are from South America?
3. Who is from the Caribbean?
4. Who is from Central America?

Answers: 1. the United States
2. María and Mateo **3.** Paco **4.** Paloma

Which Countries?

Key Terms and Phrases

Inglaterra	England
Escocia	Scotland
Irlanda	Ireland
España	Spain
Sudáfrica	South Africa

Conversation

People talking:

Soy de Inglaterra. ¿De dónde es usted?

Soy de Escocia. ¿De dónde es usted?

Soy de Irlanda. ¿De dónde es usted?

Soy de España. ¿De dónde es usted?

Soy de Sudáfrica. ¿De dónde es usted?

NOTES

The verb *ser* and its conjugations are used to state the country where somebody or something is from (see Common Irregular Verb Conjugations on page 186).

The predominantly English-speaking countries Canada and Australia are spelled the same in both English and Spanish and pronounced very similarly.

Vosotros/vosotras, not *ustedes*, is used in Spain for *you* (plural informal).

REMEMBER

Subject pronouns are not often used before the verb unless they emphasize the *who* or *what*.

Questions

1. What is the Spanish name for the Spanish-speaking country in Europe?

2. What are the Spanish names for three other European countries?

3. How do you say *South Africa* in Spanish?

Answers: 1. España   **2.** Inglaterra, Escocia, and Irlanda   **3.** Sudáfrica

Lessons 6–8

Draw a line to match the Spanish word or phrase with its English translation.

¿Hablan español?	I don't speak Spanish.
¿De dónde es?	England
No hablo español.	I speak English.
Escocia	He's from the United States.
Él es de los Estados Unidos.	Where are you (singular informal) from?
Hablo inglés.	Do you (plural) speak Spanish?
¿De dónde eres?	Scotland
Inglaterra	How do you say?
¿Cómo se dice?	Where are you (singular formal) from?

Everyday People!

Key Terms and Phrases

la niña	girl
el niño	boy
el hombre	man
los hombres	men
la mujer	woman

Conversation

PACO   Mateo y yo somos hombres.

MATEO   Sí, soy un hombre.

MARÍA   Soy una mujer.

PALOMA   Stuart y yo somos niños.

STUART   Sí, soy un niño.

PALOMA   Soy una niña.

NOTES

In Spanish, to change a noun from singular to plural, in most cases just add *s* or *es*.

All nouns are masculine or feminine in Spanish. When referring to a group that has both male and female members, the masculine plural noun is used; for example, *el niño* and *la niña* together are *los niños*.

Nouns in Spanish are often preceded by an article: feminine (*la* = *the*, *las* = *the* [plural] or *una* = *a*) or masculine (*el* = *the*, *los* = *the* [plural] or *un* = *a*).

REMEMBER

The verb *ser* is used to describe a person's inherent traits, such as ethnicity. (See Common Irregular Verb Conjugations on page 186.)

Questions

1. Who are the two *hombres*?
2. Who are the two *niños*?
3. Who is the *mujer*?
4. What does *Somos niños* mean in English?

Answers: 1. Mateo and Paco   **2.** Stuart and Paloma   **3.** María   **4.** We are children.

How's the Family?

> **REMEMBER**
> The verb *ser* is used to describe a person's inherent traits, things that cannot change, such as membership in a family.

Key Terms and Phrases

Esta es la familia de mis vecinos.	This is my neighbor's family.
¿Quiénes son todos?	Who are they all?
el padre	father
la madre	mother
el hijo	son
las hijas	daughters
los hijos	children
el hermano	brother
las hermanas	sisters

Conversation

STUART Esta es la familia de mis vecinos.

PALOMA ¿Quiénes son todos?

STUART Daniel es el padre. Susana es la madre. Alvaro es el hijo. Lorena y Paola son las hijas. Lorena, Alvaro y Paola son los hijos. Alvaro es el hermano de Lorena y Paola. Lorena y Paola son las hermanas de Alvaro. Lorena, Alvaro y Paola son hermanos.

Questions

1. Who is the *padre*?
2. Who is the *madre*?
3. Who is the *hijo*?
4. Who are the *hijas*?
5. Who are the three *hijos*?
6. Alvaro is the _____ of Lorena and Paola.
7. Lorena and Paola are the _____ of Alvaro.
8. How do you say *family* in Spanish?

Answers: 1. Daniel   2. Susana   3. Alvaro   4. Lorena and Paola   5. Lorena, Alvaro, and Paola   6. brother or hermano   7. sisters or hermanas   8. familia

How's the Rest of the Family?

> **REMEMBER**
> When a noun is plural, the singular masculine article *el* changes to *los*; for example, *el abuelo* becomes *los abuelos*. The singular feminine article *la* changes to the plural *las*; for example, *la tía* becomes *las tías*. If both genders are present, the plural defaults to the masculine, so *la tía* and *el tío* together are *los tíos*.

Key Terms and Phrases

¿Quiénes son los otros en la foto?	Who are the others in the photo?
el abuelo	grandfather
la abuela	grandmother
los abuelos	grandparents
el tío	uncle
la tía	aunt
los tíos	aunt and uncle
las primas	cousins (female)

Conversation

PALOMA ¿Quiénes son los otros en la foto?

STUART Luis y Ana son los abuelos de Lorena, Alvaro y Paola. Claudia y David son los tíos de Lorena, Alvaro y Paola. Alba y Blanca son sus primas.

> **NOTES**
> Usually in Spanish if a noun ends in *o* it is masculine, whereas nouns that end in *a* are feminine. There are exceptions though!

Questions

1. Who is the *abuelo*?
2. Who is the *abuela*?
3. Who is the *tía* of Lorena, Alvaro, and Paola?
4. Who is their *tío*?
5. Who are their *primas*?

Answers: 1. Luis   2. Ana   3. Claudia   4. David   5. Alba and Blanca

Do You Have a Pet?

> **REMEMBER**
> To make a statement negative, simply put *no*
> in front of the verb; for example, *No tengo*
> (*I do not have*).

Key Terms and Phrases

la mascota	pet
el perro	dog
el gato	cat
el conejo	rabbit
el pájaro	bird
tengo	I have
tienes	you (informal) have
tiene	he/she has, or you (formal) have

> **NOTES**
> The verb conjugation of *tener* can be found
> in Common Irregular Verb Conjugations on
> page 186.

Conversation

STUART Tengo un perro. Paloma, ¿tienes una mascota?

PALOMA Sí, tengo un gato. Stuart, ¿tienes un conejo?

STUART No tengo un conejo. Mateo tiene un conejo.

MARÍA Tengo una mascota también. Tengo un pájaro.

> **Questions**
>
> 1. Who has a *pájaro*?
> 2. Who has a *perro*?
> 3. Who says he doesn't have a *conejo*?
> 4. Who does have a *conejo*?
> 5. To whom does the *gato* belong?

Answers: 1. María 2. Stuart 3. Stuart 4. Mateo 5. Paloma

Lessons 9–12

Translate the following sentences from English to Spanish.

1. Paloma is a girl and a daughter. _____

    _____

2. Stuart is a boy and a son. _____

    _____

3. Daniel is a man and a father. _____

    _____

4. Susana is a woman and a mother. _____

    _____

5. Claudia is a sister and an aunt. _____

    _____

6. David is a brother and an uncle. _____

    _____

7. Luis is a grandfather. _____

    _____

8. Ana is a grandmother. _____

    _____

9. The children are cousins. _____

    _____

10. The family has pets. _____

    _____

Fill in each blank with the pet name in Spanish that makes the most sense.

11. The _____ barks.

12. The _____ meows.

13. The _____ flies.

14. The _____ hops.

Describe Them!

> **REMEMBER**
> The verb *ser* is used when describing more permanent traits of a person or thing. (See Common Irregular Verb Conjugations on page 186.)

Key Terms and Phrases

alto	tall
bajo	short
guapo	handsome (male)
guapa	pretty (female)
guapos	handsome/pretty (plural)
viejo	old
joven	young

Conversation

Mateo es alto y María es baja. Paloma es guapa. Stuart es guapo. Stuart y Paloma son guapos. Paco es viejo y Paloma es joven.

> **NOTES**
> Adjectives, like nouns, are masculine or feminine and must agree with the noun they are describing. For example, *Mateo* (male) *es alto*, but *María* (female) *es baja*.
>
> And because Stuart and Paloma are both nice-looking, the adjective must be plural to match the plural subject; therefore, *Stuart y Paloma son guapos*.

Questions

1. Who is *joven*?
2. Who is *viejo*?
3. Who are *guapos*?
4. Who is *alto*?
5. Who is *baja*?

Answers: 1. Paloma   2. Paco   3. Stuart and Paloma   4. Mateo   5. María

Describe Them More!

Key Terms and Phrases

cansado/a	tired
casado/a	married
soltero/a	single
despierto/a	awake
ocupado/a	busy
después	later

Conversation

STUART Yo estoy cansado. ¿Y tú, Paloma, estás cansada?

PALOMA ¡Estoy despierta! ¿Hablamos después, Stuart?

STUART Estoy ocupado hoy.

PACO Yo no estoy casado. Estoy soltero. ¿Ustedes están casados, Mateo y María?

MATEO AND MARÍA Sí, estamos casados.

NOTES

Mateo and María, who are talking, use just the verb *estamos* and not the subject pronoun *nosotros*. It is not necessary to use the subject pronoun because *we* is implied by the verb conjugation.

Paco is talking to María and Mateo, so he uses *ustedes* (*you* plural), although it's not necessary because *you* is implied by the verb conjugation.

REMEMBER

The verb *estar* is used when describing temporary states of a person or thing. (See Common Irregular Verb Conjugations on page 186.)

Questions

1. Who is single?
2. Which two people are married?
3. Who is tired?
4. Who is busy?
5. Who is awake?

Answers: 1. Paco **2.** Mateo and María **3.** Stuart **4.** Stuart **5.** Paloma

Describe Them Even More!

Key Terms and Phrases

la sed	thirst
el hambre	hunger
la suerte	luck
el calor	heat
el frío	cold

Conversation

STUART AND PALOMA Tenemos calor y sed.

PACO Tengo hambre y frío.

MATEO ¡Tengo suerte!

> **NOTES**
>
> In English, the verb *to be* is used to describe certain states of being, such as in the phrases *I am hungry* or *He is cold*. In Spanish, these certain states of being use the verb *tener*, which means *to have*. The literal translation is *I have hunger*, *He has cold*, and so on.
>
> The verb *tener* and its conjugations can be found in Common Irregular Verb Conjugations on page 186.

Questions

1. What are the Spanish words to describe how Stuart and Paloma are feeling?

2. What is the Spanish word to describe how Mateo is feeling?

3. What are the Spanish words to describe how Paco is feeling?

4. Who is feeling cold?

Answers: 1. calor, sed 2. suerte 3. hambre, frío 4. Paco

What Colors Do You Like?

REMEMBER

When colors are used as adjectives, they must agree with their subject. For example, the singular masculine noun *carro* (*car*) uses the singular masculine adjective *negro* (*black*) to describe it. The singular feminine noun *casa* (*house*) uses the singular feminine adjective *blanca* (*white*) to describe it. *Carros* are described as *negros*, whereas *casas* are described as *blancas*.

When a color is used as a solitary noun (and doesn't describe something), it uses the masculine article *el*.

Key Terms and Phrases

el amarillo	yellow
el azul	blue
el blanco	white
el negro	black
el marrón, el café	brown
el morado	purple
el rojo	red
el verde	green
el color/los colores	color/colors
¿Cuál?	Which?
gustar	to like

Conversation

MATEO   ¿Cuáles colores te gustan?

MARÍA   Me gusta el rojo. A Paloma le gusta el morado.

PALOMA No me gusta el morado. Me gusta el verde.

STUART   Me gusta el café porque tengo un perro café. También me gusta el azul.

MATEO   Paco, ¿cuáles colores le gustan?

PACO   Me gusta el amarillo. También me gustan el blanco y el negro porque tengo un gato con estos colores.

CONTINUED

NOTES

Unlike in English, the adjective is often placed after the noun in Spanish. *The brown dog* in Spanish is *el perro café* ("the dog brown").

Brown can be translated as *marrón* or *café* depending on the country.

The verb *gustar* means *to like*, but it literally translates to "being pleased."

Gustar is an atypical verb in Spanish because its sentence structure is not like most other verbs. When using the verb *gustar*, the subject (the thing that is pleasing) comes *after* the conjugated form of *gustar,* and the sentence *starts* with an object pronoun (which refers to the person being pleased). For example, *Me gusta la pizza* (*I like pizza*), but the literal translation is "The pizza pleases me." *Le gusta la pizza* (*He or she likes pizza*) literally translates to "The pizza pleases him or her."

If it's a *plural* subject that's doing the pleasing, add an *n* after *gusta*. For example, *Me gustan las pizzas* (*I like the pizzas*), *Te gustan las pizzas* (*You like the pizzas*), *Les gustan las pizzas* (*They or you (plural) like the pizzas*), and so on.

Questions

1. What is the word in Spanish for the color María likes?

2. What is the word in Spanish for the color Paloma likes?

3. What are the words in Spanish for the two colors Stuart likes?

4. What is the word in Spanish for the color Paloma does not like?

5. What are the words in Spanish for the three colors Paco likes?

6. Why do Stuart and Paco like the colors brown, black, and white?

Answers: 1. el rojo   **2.** el verde   **3.** el café and el azul   **4.** el morado
5. el amarillo, el blanco, and el negro   **6.** Because those are the colors of their pets.

Describe It!

> **REMEMBER**
>
> The verb *ser* (*to be*) is used to describe a more or less permanent or non-changing characteristic of a thing or person.
>
> Adjectives must agree in gender (masculine or feminine) and number (singular or plural) with the noun or nouns being described.

Key Terms and Phrases

grande	big
pequeño	small
viejo	old
nuevo	new
caro	expensive
barato	inexpensive

Conversation

Los Estados Unidos es grande. Puerto Rico es pequeño. La casa blanca es vieja. La casa de María es nueva. El carro de Paco es caro. El carro de Mateo es barato.

CONTINUED

> **NOTES**
>
> Spanish doesn't use 's to show possession, as in *María's house*. Instead, *la casa de María* (*the house of María*) is the correct usage.
>
> In Spain and some other countries, the term *el coche* is used for *car* and is masculine. For example, *El coche es nuevo* (*The car is new*).

Questions

1. Which country is *grande*?
2. Which is the old house?
3. Which is the new house?
4. Who has the expensive car?
5. Who has the inexpensive car?

Answers: 1. The United States or Los Estados Unidos   **2.** la casa blanca   **3.** la casa de María   **4.** Paco   **5.** Mateo

Lessons 13–17

Write the opposite of the following words.

1. alto _____

2. caro _____

3. cansado _____

4. casado _____

5. grande _____

6. calor _____

7. How do you write *He is busy* in Spanish? _____

8. Translate this sentence from Spanish to English: *Paloma es guapa.* _____
   _____

9. Translate this sentence from Spanish to English: *Mateo tiene suerte.* _____
   _____

10. What is the word in Spanish for both an old person and an old thing? _____
    _____

11. If you go to a restaurant, you are probably feeling which two words in Spanish?
    _____   _____

12. Which two color adjectives describe a zebra in Spanish? (*Cebra* is a feminine noun.)
    _____   _____

CONTINUED

Match the following Spanish sentences with their English equivalents.

¿Cuáles colores les gustan?	He likes blue.
Le gusta el azul.	Which colors do you (plural) like?
Le gusta el verde.	The dog is brown.
Me gusta el rojo.	I don't like purple.
¿Te gusta el amarillo?	I like red.
El perro es café.	Do you (singular informal) like yellow?
No me gusta el morado.	She likes green.

Whose Is It?

Key Terms and Phrases

mi	my
tu	your (singular informal)
su	his, hers, your (singular formal), your (plural)
nuestro/a	our
el país	country
el ciudadano/ la ciudadana	citizen
el territorio	territory
por eso	for that reason

Conversation

STUART Los Estados Unidos es mi país. Paraguay es su país, Mateo.

PACO Costa Rica es tu país, Paloma. Y Chile es su país, María.

PACO Puerto Rico es un territorio de los Estados Unidos y, por eso, soy un ciudadano Americano.

MATEO Todos nuestros países son buenos.

NOTES

Possessive adjectives must agree in both gender and number (singular or plural) with the noun being described. For example, *Los Estados Unidos es mi país* (*The United States is my country*, singular, one country) and *Los Estados Unidos es nuestro país* (*The United States is our country*, still singular, one country). *Los Estados Unidos y Paraguay son nuestros países* (*The United States and Paraguay are our countries*, plural, more than one country).

In Spain, *vuestro(s)/vuestra(s)* (*your* plural informal) is used as the possessive adjective along with *su* (*your* singular or plural formal).

CONTINUED

REMEMBER

The verb *ser* (to be) is used to describe a non-changing characteristic of a thing or person.

Questions

1. In Spanish, what does Paco tell Paloma?

2. In Spanish, what does Paco tell María?

3. In Spanish, what does Mateo tell everyone?

4. Is Paco a U.S. citizen?

Answers: 1. Costa Rica es tu país.   2. Chile es su país.   3. Todos nuestros países son buenos.   4. Yes.

What's Your Phone Number?

Key Terms and Phrases

¿Cuál es su número de teléfono?	What's your (formal) phone number?
Mi número es . . .	My number is . . .
¿Cuál es el número de teléfono de Stuart?	What is Stuart's phone number?
¿Cuál es el código del país?	What is the country code?
por favor	please
para llamar	to call
fuera	outside
marque	dial (formal)

Conversation

MARÍA   Mi número es 508-2009. ¿Cuál es el número de teléfono de Stuart?

PACO   El número de Stuart es 315-2007. María, ¿cuál es el código del país?

MARÍA   El código para llamar a Chile es 56. Para llamar fuera de los Estados Unidos, marque 011.

> **NOTES**
> For the pronunciation of numbers 0 to 1,000, see Numbers: Los Números on page 188.
>   Some people say each individual number when giving a telephone number, whereas others might group certain numbers. For example, *3-8-3-4-5-3-2* (*tres, ocho, tres, cuatro, cinco, tres, dos*) or *3-8-3-45-32* (*tres, ocho, tres, cuarenta y cinco, treinta y dos*).

CONTINUED

REMEMBER

The verb *ser* is used when stating phone numbers.

Questions

1. What is María's phone number?

2. What is the *código del país* for Chile?

3. What must one dial to call outside the United States?

Answers: 1. 508-2009   2. 56   3. 011

What's Your Address?

Key Terms and Phrases

¿Cuál es su dirección?	What's your address? (formal)
Mi dirección es . . .	My address is . . .
¿Cuál es la dirección del restaurante?	What's the restaurant's address?
Nuestra dirección es . . .	Our address is . . .
la calle	street
en frente de	across the street from
al lado de	next to
detrás de	behind

Conversation

MATEO Paco, ¿cuál es su dirección, por favor?

PACO Mi dirección es 2935 Avenida Fierro, en frente del parque. ¿Y ustedes, cuál es su dirección?

MARÍA AND MATEO Nuestra dirección es 624 Calle Talavera, al lado de una casa amarilla.

PACO Gracias, ¿cuál es la dirección del restaurante Tapas de Miguel?

MATEO ¡El restaurante está detrás de mi casa!

REMEMBER

The possessive adjective *tu* (*your*) is singular informal. The possessive adjective *su* can be (1) *your* (singular formal), (2) *your* (plural), or (3) *his* or *her*.

The verb *ser* is used when stating addresses.

Questions

1. What is Paco's address?

2. Where is the park in relation to Paco's house?

3. What is Mateo and María's street name?

Answers: 1. 2935 Avenida Fierro   2. It is in front of Paco's house.   3. Talavera

Through the Ages

Key Terms and Phrases

¿Cuántos años tienen ustedes?	How old are you (plural)?
¿Cuántos años tienes?	How old are you (singular informal)?
Tenemos 33 años.	We are 33 years old.
Tengo 33 años.	I'm 33 years old.
Ella tiene 10 años.	She is 10 years old.

Conversation

PACO   ¿Cuántos años tienen ustedes?

MATEO   Tengo 33 años.

MARÍA   Yo también. Tengo 33 años. Mateo y yo tenemos 33 años.

PACO   Y Paloma, ¿cuántos años tiene ella?

MARÍA   Ella tiene 10 años. Stuart tiene 12 años.

Questions

1. ¿Cuántos años tiene Paloma?
2. ¿Cuántos años tienen Mateo y María?
3. ¿Cuántos años tiene Stuart?

Answers: 1. 10   2. 33   3. 12

NOTES

The verb *tener* is used for stating the age of something or someone, like a possession. Paloma "has 10 years" instead of "is 10 years old," as in English.

The verb *tener* and its conjugations can be found in Common Irregular Verb Conjugations on page 186.

Lessons 18–21

Fill in each blank with the appropriate possessive adjective.

| mi | tu | su | nuestro | nuestros |
| mis | tus | sus | nuestra | nuestras |

1. Daniel tiene gatos. _____ gatos son negros y blancos.

2. ¿Cuál es _____ dirección, niño? (adult talking to a child)

3. _____ nombre es Anna. (person talking to another person about Anna)

4. Mateo, _____ dirección está al lado de la casa amarilla. (María talking to Mateo; they live together)

5. "_____ país es México." (a man telling a woman about his country of origin)

Fill in each blank with the key term or phrase that makes the most sense.

| código del país | tiene | número de teléfono | ciudadano | dirección |

6. Paco es de Puerto Rico. Paco es un _____ de los Estados Unidos.

7. Para llamar fuera de los Estados Unidos, marque 011 y despúes el _____.

8. 56-794-7624 es mi _____.

9. Nuestra _____ es 2935 Calle Talavera.

10. Patricio _____ 18 años.

Time: Days, Weeks, and Seasons

What a Day!

Key Terms and Phrases

¿Qué día es?	What day is it?
hoy	today
mañana	tomorrow
el lunes	Monday
el martes	Tuesday
el miércoles	Wednesday
el jueves	Thursday
el viernes	Friday
entonces	then

Conversation

PALOMA ¿Qué día es hoy?

STUART Hoy es miércoles.

PALOMA No es miércoles. Mañana es miércoles.

STUART ¡Entonces hoy es martes!

NOTES
Days of the week in English are always capitalized. In Spanish, they are capitalized only when used at the beginning of a sentence. For example, *Hoy es lunes* (Today is Monday), but *Lunes es mañana* (Monday is tomorrow).

Mañana means both *tomorrow* and *morning* in Spanish.

REMEMBER
The verb *ser* (*to be*) is used to state non-changing/permanent situations or descriptors, such as the days of the week; for example, *Hoy es lunes* (Today is Monday).

Questions

1. At the end of the conversation, what day does Stuart say it is?

2. What day will tomorrow be?

3. If today is Tuesday, what day was yesterday?

4. How do you translate both *tomorrow* and *morning* into Spanish?

Answers: 1. martes   **2.** miércoles   **3.** lunes   **4.** mañana

Hooray for the Weekend!

Key Terms and Phrases

el fin de semana	weekend
el sábado	Saturday
el domingo	Sunday
¿Por qué?	Why?
Porque tengo más tiempo	Because I have more time

Conversation

PALOMA ¡Me gusta el fin de semana!

STUART A mí también. Me gusta el sábado más que el domingo.

PALOMA ¿Por qué?

STUART Porque tengo más tiempo con mis amigos el sábado.

PALOMA A mí me gusta más el domingo.

Questions

1. Which day does Stuart prefer?

2. Why does he prefer that day?

3. Which day does Paloma prefer?

Answers: 1. el sábado   2. Porque tiene más tiempo con sus amigos.   3. el domingo

What Time Is It (a.m.)?

REMEMBER
The verb *ser* (*to be*) is used to tell the time; for example, *Son las nueve. = It's 9:00 a.m.* Refer to Numbers: Los Números on page 188 for number review and pronunciation.

Key Terms and Phrases

¿Qué hora es?	What time is it?
Son las seis.	It's six o'clock.
Son las siete y cuarto.	It's 7:15.
Son las ocho y media.	It's 8:30.
Falta un cuarto para las once.	It's 10:45.
Son las once y cinco.	It's 11:05.
tener razón	to be correct
estar seguro/a	to be sure
creer	to believe

Conversation

MATEO ¿Qué hora es, María?

MARÍA Son las seis, Mateo. No, no tengo razón. Son las siete y cuarto.

MATEO ¿Estás segura? Creo que son las ocho y media.

MARÍA ¿Estás seguro? Creo que falta un cuarto para las once.

MATEO No tienes razón, María. ¡Estoy seguro que son las once y cinco!

CONTINUED

NOTES

Spanish does not normally use an equivalent of the term o'clock; instead, just say *Es la una, son las dos*, and so on.

Questions

1. How do you say *What time is it?*

2. Write out the words *It is 6:00.*

3. Write out the words *It is 7:15.*

4. Write out the words *It is 8:30.*

5. Write out the words *It is 10:45.*

Answers: 1. ¿Qué hora es?   **2.** Son las seis.   **3.** Son las siete y cuarto.   **4.** Son las ocho y media.   **5.** Falta un cuarto para las once.

What Time Is It (p.m.)?

Key Terms and Phrases

Son las doce.	It's 12:00.
Es mediodía.	It's noon.
Es la una.	It's 1:00.
Son las dos.	It's 2:00.
Son las tres.	It's 3:00.
Son las cuatro.	It's 4:00.
Son las nueve.	It's 9:00.

Conversation

MATEO ¿Qué hora es, María, en Tijuana, México?

MARÍA Son las doce, o mediodía . ¿Qué hora es, Mateo, en Juárez, México?

MATEO Es la una en Juárez. ¿Qué hora es, María, en Zacatecas, México?

MARÍA Son las dos. ¿Qué hora es, Mateo, en la República Dominicana?

MATEO Son las tres. ¿Qué hora es, María, en Buenos Aires, Argentina?

MARÍA Son las cuatro. ¿Qué hora es, Mateo, en España?

MATEO Son las nueve.

NOTES

La una (1:00–1:59) is the only singular number for telling time; therefore, use *es* (*is*) instead of *son* (*are*).

Also use singular *es* when using the term *mediodía* (*noon*).

Questions

1. What time is it in Spain?

2. What time is it in the Dominican Republic?

3. What time is it in Tijuana, Mexico?

4. What time is it in Buenos Aires, Argentina?

5. What time is it in Juárez, Mexico?

Answers: 1. Son las nueve. 2. Son las tres. 3. Son las doce or Es mediodía. 4. Son las cuatro. 5. Es la una.

What Time Do You Do That (a.m.)?

REMEMBER
Between adults, *usted* is used until people are familiar with each other. Because María and Mateo are married, they use *tú*. Even though María and Mateo have become friends with Paco, they continue to use *usted* because he is older and they want to show him respect.

Key Terms and Phrases

¿A qué hora . . . ?	At what time . . . ?
levantarse	to wake up
vestirse	to get dressed
desayunar	to eat breakfast
ir a la escuela	to go to school
almorzar	to eat lunch

Conversation

MATEO ¿A qué hora se levanta, Paco?

PACO: A las 7:00. ¿A qué hora se levantan ustedes, Mateo y María?

MARÍA Nos levantamos a las 6:00. ¿A qué hora te vistes, Paloma?

PALOMA Me visto a las 7:30. ¿A qué hora desayunas, Stuart?

STUART Desayuno a las 7:45. ¿A qué hora vas a la escuela, Paloma?

PALOMA Voy a la escuela a las 8:15. ¿A qué hora almuerza, Paco?

PACO Almuerzo al mediodía.

NOTES

In Mexico, the verb *lonchear* is more common than *almorzar*.

For *-ar*, *-er*, and *-ir* verb conjugations, see Regular Verb Conjugations on page 185.

Reflexive verbs like *levantarse* and *vestirse* use reflexive pronouns to indicate that someone or something is performing an action on or for himself/herself/itself. Many actions related to personal care or daily routines are reflexive.

The four reflexive pronouns are:

me = I

te = you (singular informal)

se = you (singular formal), *you* (plural), and *he/she/it*

nos = we

In Spain, the reflexive pronoun *os* is used instead of *se* when using *you* plural informal.

Questions

1. What does Paco do at 7:00?

2. What do Mateo and María do at 6:00?

3. What does Paloma do at 7:30?

4. What does Stuart do at 7:45?

5. What does Paloma do at 8:15?

6. What does Paco do at noon?

Answers: 1. He gets up. **2.** They get up. **3.** She gets dressed. **4.** He eats breakfast. **5.** She goes to school. **6.** He eats lunch.

What Time Do You Do That (p.m.)?

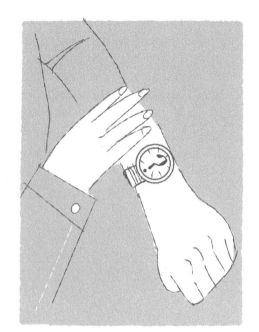

Key Terms and Phrases

llegar a casa	to come home
cenar	to eat dinner
ir a la cama	to go to bed

Conversation

MATEO ¿A qué hora llegas a la casa de la escuela, Paloma?

PALOMA A las 3:00. ¿A qué hora cenan ustedes, Mateo y María?

MARÍA Cenamos a las 6:00. ¿A qué hora vas a la cama, Stuart?

STUART A las 9:00 de la noche.

NOTES

In many Spanish-speaking countries, the 24-hour clock is used. Stuart could say he goes to bed at 21:00 instead of 9:00.

Questions

1. What does Paloma do at 3:00?

2. What do Mateo and María do at 6:00?

3. What does Stuart do at 9:00?

Answers: 1. She comes home from school. **2.** They eat dinner. **3.** He goes to bed.

Lessons 22–27

Fill in each blank with the best key term.

| sábado | mañana | mediodía | jueves | domingo |

1. If *domingo* is *hoy*, *lunes* is _____.

2. If *mañana* is *viernes*, what day is *hoy*? _____

3. What two days are the *fin de semana*? _____ _____

4. When do many people *almorzar*? _____

Verdadero o Falso = True or False

Put a *V* for true statements and an *F* for false statements.

5. To make a statement negative in Spanish, place *no* in front of the verb. _____

6. It is common in Spanish to use the term *o'clock*. _____

7. The verb *estar* is used to tell the day and time. _____

Fill in each blank with the correct reflexive pronoun: *me, te, se,* or *nos.*

(8)_____ levantamos a las 8:00 pero Paloma (9) _____ levanta a las 9:00 los fines de semana. (10) _____ levanto a las 6:00 los lunes. Y tú, ¿a qué hora (11) _____ levantas?

Match the activity with an appropriate time.

Nos levantamos	a las 7:15.
Vamos a la escuela	a las 7:00.
Nos vestimos	a las 6:45.
Desayunamos en casa	a las 8:00.

'Tis the Summer Season

Key Terms and Phrases

el verano	summer
junio	June
julio	July
agosto	August
¿Qué mes es?	What month is it?
la mejor estación	the best season

Conversation

STUART Me gusta el verano. ¡Es la mejor estación!
¿Qué mes es?

PALOMA Es junio. Julio es después de junio.

STUART Sí, y agosto es después de julio.

NOTES

This lesson is referring to summer in temperate zones in the Northern Hemisphere.

Unless used as the first word of a sentence, neither the months nor the seasons are capitalized in Spanish.

The verb *ser* is used to state the month.

The term *temporada* is also used for *season*.

Questions

1. What month is *después de junio*?

2. What month is *después de julio*?

3. What month does Paloma say it is now?

4. Summer is Stuart's favorite _____.

Answers: 1. julio   2. agosto   3. junio   4. estación

'Tis the Autumn Season

Key Terms and Phrases

el otoño	autumn/fall
septiembre	September
octubre	October
noviembre	November

Conversation

MATEO Me gusta el otoño. ¡Es la mejor estación! ¿Qué mes es?

MARÍA Es septiembre. Octubre es después de septiembre.

MATEO Sí, y noviembre es después de octubre.

NOTES

This lesson is referring to autumn in temperate zones in the Northern Hemisphere.

Questions

1. What month is *después de septiembre*?
2. What month is *después de octubre*?
3. What month does María say it is now?
4. Which season is Mateo's favorite?

Answers: 1. octubre   2. noviembre   3. septiembre   4. el otoño

'Tis the Winter Season

Key Terms and Phrases

el invierno	winter
diciembre	December
enero	January
febrero	February
la peor estación	the worst season

Conversation

PACO No me gusta el invierno. ¡Es la peor estación! ¿Qué mes es?

MATEO Es diciembre. Enero es después de diciembre.

PACO Sí, y febrero es después de enero.

NOTES

This lesson is referring to winter in temperate zones in the Northern Hemisphere.

Questions

1. What month is *después de diciembre*?

2. What month is *después de enero*?

3. What month does Mateo say it is now?

4. Which season is Paco's least favorite?

Answers: 1. enero   **2.** febrero   **3.** diciembre   **4.** el invierno

'Tis the Spring Season

Key Terms and Phrases

la primavera	spring
marzo	March
abril	April
mayo	May

Conversation

PALOMA Me gusta la primavera. ¡Es la mejor estación! ¿Qué mes es?

MARÍA Es marzo. Abril es después de marzo.

PALOMA Sí, y mayo es después de abril.

> **NOTES**
> This lesson is referring to spring in temperate zones in the Northern Hemisphere.

Questions

1. What month is *después de marzo*?

2. What month is *después de abril*?

3. What month does María say it is now?

4. Which season is Paloma's favorite?

Answers: 1. abril   2. mayo   3. marzo   4. la primavera

Singing in the Rainy Season

Key Terms and Phrases

la temporada de lluvias	the rainy season
un paraguas	an umbrella
¿Cuáles son los meses de . . . ?	What are the months of . . . ?

Conversation

STUART Es la temporada de lluvias.

PACO Sí, tengo un paraguas para nosotros.

STUART ¿Cuáles son los meses de la temporada de lluvias en Guatemala?

PACO Son junio, julio, agosto, septiembre y octubre.

NOTES

The term *la sombrilla* may also be used for *umbrella*.

Countries in tropical zones have two seasons: rainy and dry.

Questions

1. What season is it?

2. What is Paco carrying?

3. What month does the rainy season begin in Guatemala?

4. What month does the rainy season end in Guatemala?

Answers: 1. la temporada de lluvias   2. un paraguas   3. junio   4. octubre

Let's Talk About the Weather

Key Terms and Phrases

Hace calor.	It's hot.
Hace frío.	It's cold.
Hace viento.	It's windy.
Está lloviendo.	It's raining.
Está nevando.	It's snowing.

Conversation

STUART Hace calor.

PACO Hace frío.

MARÍA Hace viento.

PALOMA Está lloviendo.

MATEO Está nevando.

> **NOTES**
> The verb *estar* is used for present progressive—when something is happening right this moment.

Questions

1. What does Paco say?

2. What does Mateo say?

3. What does Paloma say?

4. What does María say?

5. What does Stuart say?

Answers: 1. Hace frío. 2. Está nevando. 3. Está lloviendo. 4. Hace viento. 5. Hace calor.

What's the Date?

Key Terms and Phrases

¿Cuál es la fecha?	What's the date?
Es el 20 de marzo.	It's March 20.
Es el primer día de primavera.	It's the first day of spring.
¿Cuándo es el primer día de verano?	When is the first day of summer?

Conversation

PALOMA ¿Cuál es la fecha de hoy?

STUART Es el 20 de marzo. Es el primer día de primavera.

PALOMA ¿Cuándo es el primer día de verano?

STUART Es el 21 de junio.

NOTES

Use the verb *ser* when stating the date.

In Spanish, the date precedes the month, as in *el 20 de marzo,* whereas in English, the date follows the month, as in *March 20*. If someone from a Spanish-speaking country tells you her birthday is *5-8-2000*, she was born on August 5, not May 8.

In English, numbers for stating the date are ordinal (tell the position or order of something). In Spanish, it is more common to use cardinal numbers to give the date. However, use the ordinal number *primer* (*the first*) when referring to the first day of the month.

REMEMBER

Numbers and their pronunciations can be found in Numbers: Los Números on page 188.

Questions

1. What does Paloma first ask Stuart?

2. What is special about this date?

3. What is the second question Paloma asks Stuart?

4. How does Stuart respond?

5. What is today's date in the conversation?

Answers: 1. ¿Cuál es la fecha? **2.** Es el primer día de primavera. **3.** ¿Cuándo es el primer día de verano? **4.** Es el 21 de junio. **5.** Es el 20 de marzo.

Lessons 28–34

These months are referring to seasons in the Northern Hemisphere. Write the answers in Spanish.

1. Write one of the months in *la primavera*. _____

2. In which season would you most likely say *Hace calor*? _____

3. Which month is the first month of the year? _____

4. Which month is the last month of the year? _____

5. In which season would you most likely say *Hace frío*? _____

6. In which season do the leaves fall? _____

7. If *está lloviendo*, what object would you want to have with you? _____

8. *¿Cuál es la fecha del primer día en el año nuevo?* _____

9. In Central America, the Caribbean, and other tropical regions, the rainy season
   is called _____.

10. If the wind is strong, what might you say? _____

Write the following dates in Spanish. Example: April 26: el 26 de abril.

11. March 15 _____

12. May 10 _____

13. February 7 _____

14. August 1 _____

Emotions, Health, and Wellness

57

What a Great Feeling!

> **REMEMBER**
>
> The verb *estar* is used when describing impermanent emotions. (See Common Irregular Verb Conjugations on page 186.)
>
> Adjectives are masculine or feminine and must agree in both gender and number (singular or plural) with the noun they are describing. For example, *Mateo está listo* and *María está lista* but *Mateo and María están listos*.

Key Terms and Phrases

feliz	happy
bien	well
orgulloso	proud
emocionado	excited
listo	ready
muy	very

Questions

1. What does Mateo ask Paloma?
2. How does María feel about Paloma?
3. What does Stuart ask Paloma?
4. What is the adjective to describe that Paloma feels excited?

Answers: 1. ¿Estás lista? **2.** orgulloso **3.** ¿Estás feliz? **4.** emocionada

Conversation

MATEO ¿Estás lista, Paloma?

PALOMA ¡Sí! Estoy lista y emocionada.

MARÍA Estamos orgullosos de tí, Paloma.

STUART ¿Estás feliz, Paloma?

PALOMA Sí, estoy muy bien.

What a Not-So-Great Feeling!

Key Terms and Phrases

infeliz	unhappy
mal	bad, wrong, or not feeling well
triste	sad
enojado	angry
aburrido	bored
la nota	grade
el libro	book
¿Qué te pasa?	What's wrong? (informal)
No te preocupes.	Don't worry. (informal)

Conversation

MATEO   ¿Qué te pasa, Stuart?

STUART   Estoy infeliz porque mi nota no salió bien.
¿Está enojado?

MATEO   No te preocupes. No estoy enojado.

PACO   No me gusta el libro. Estoy aburrido.

MARÍA   Estoy triste que a Paco no le gusta el libro.

Questions

1. How does Stuart feel about his grade?

2. How do you describe Stuart's grade?

3. How does Paco feel about the book?

4. How does María feel about Paco's boredom
   with the book?

Answers: 1. infeliz   2. mala   3. aburrido   4. triste

Lessons 35–36

Match the adjective with the noun(s) it describes according to gender and number.

Paco está	emocionada.
Stuart y Paco están	listas.
Paloma está	aburridos.
Nosotras estamos	enojado.

Write the opposite of the following adjectives.

1. feliz _____

2. bien _____

3. emocionado _____

What is an appropriate response, in Spanish, to the following situations?

4. Someone looks upset. You ask the question _____
_____

5. You are getting a ride home from school, and you want to tell the person you are ready.
You say _____
_____

6. The person giving you a ride asks if you mind waiting just a minute. You tell this friend
_____.

Translate the following sentences from English to Spanish.

7. We are well. _____

8. They are sad. _____

When You Can't Keep the Doctor Away: Oh, My Head!

Key Terms and Phrases

¿Qué le pasa?	What's wrong (formal)?
¿Dónde le duele?	Where does it hurt (formal)?
Me duele el/la . . .	My . . . hurts.
la garganta	throat
la nariz	nose
la cabeza	head
las orejas	ears
los ojos	eyes

Conversation

DOCTOR Buenos días, ¿qué le pasa? ¿Dónde le duele?

MARÍA Me duele la cabeza.

DOCTOR ¿Le duele la garganta también?

MARÍA No me duele la garganta. Me duele la cabeza.

DOCTOR ¿Le duelen las orejas y la nariz también?

MARÍA ¡Sí! Y me duelen los ojos.

NOTES

The verb and noun must agree in number. For example, since *throat* is singular, we say *Me duele la garganta* (*My throat hurts me*). Because *ears* is plural, we say *Me duelen las orejas* (*My ears hurt me*).

Questions

1. What are the first two questions the doctor asks María?

2. What part of María's head does not hurt?

3. Which three parts of María's head *do* hurt?

Answers: 1. ¿Qué le pasa? and ¿Dónde le duele? **2.** la garganta **3.** las orejas, la nariz, los ojos

When You Can't Keep the Doctor Away: Other Health Problems

Key Terms and Phrases

el pecho	chest
el corazón	heart
la espalda	back
el estómago	stomach
la mano	hand
el brazo	arm
la pierna	leg
el pie/los pies	foot/feet
Me gustaría escuchar . . .	I'd like to listen to . . .
la diarrea	diarrhea
Tome esta medicina.	Take this medicine. (formal)

Conversation

DOCTOR Buenos días. ¿Dónde le duele?

MATEO Me duele el pecho.

DOCTOR Me gustaría escuchar su corazón. ¿Le duele la espalda?

MATEO No.

DOCTOR Buenos días. ¿Dónde le duele?

PACO Me duele el estómago. Tengo diarrea.

DOCTOR Tome esta medicina.

DOCTOR Buenos días. ¿Dónde te duele?

PALOMA Me duele la pierna y el pie.

DOCTOR ¿Te duele el brazo? ¿Te duele la mano?

PALOMA No me duele el brazo. No me duele la mano.

REMEMBER

The doctor uses *te duele* with Paloma because she's a child and uses *le duele* with each of the adults.

Questions

1. What is hurting Mateo, and what is not hurting him?

2. What is hurting Paco, and what does he have?

3. What two parts are hurting Paloma?

4. What two parts are not hurting Paloma?

Answers: 1. Le duele el pecho. No le duele la espalda. 2. Le duele el estómago. Tiene diarrea. 3. Le duelen la pierna y el pie. 4. No le duele el brazo. No le duele la mano.

At the Dentist

Key Terms and Phrases

el/la dentista	dentist
Abre la boca	Open your (informal) mouth.
el cepillo de dientes	toothbrush
la pasta dental	toothpaste
cepillarse los dientes	to brush one's teeth
las caries	cavities
le gustaría tener (o pedir) una cita	would like to make an appointment
Me alegro.	I'm glad.
Nos vemos.	We'll see each other.

Conversation

DENTISTA Abre la boca, por favor.

STUART ¿Tengo caries?

DENTISTA No tienes caries. Te cepillas bien los dientes.

STUART Me alegro. A mi madre le gustaría tener (o pedir) una cita en seis meses.

DENTISTA Muy bien. Aquí están pasta dental y un cepillo de dientes.

STUART Nos vemos en seis meses.

Questions

1. Why doesn't Stuart have cavities?
2. What does Stuart's mom want to do in six months?
3. What two items does the dentist give Stuart?
4. What does Stuart say to the dentist before leaving?

Answers: 1. Porque se cepilla bien los dientes. 2. Le gustaría tener (o pedir) una cita. 3. pasta dental y un cepillo de dientes 4. Nos vemos en seis meses.

Lessons 37–39

Answer the following questions in Spanish.

1. What are two common questions the doctor might ask you?

    _____

    _____

2. If you want to make an appointment, what do you say? _____

    _____

3. What does the dentist ask you to open? _____

4. What do you put on your toothbrush before brushing your teeth? _____

5. When the dentist tells you that you have no cavities, how would you say *I'm glad*?

    _____

6. You chew with your _____.

7. You wave to someone with your _____.

8. You swallow with your _____.

9. You put your shoe on your _____.

10. You smell with your _____.

CONTINUED

Match the body part in Spanish to its English translation.

las orejas	chest
el pecho	back
la espalda	ears
el corazón	arm
la cabeza	heart
el estómago	head
el brazo	leg
la pierna	stomach

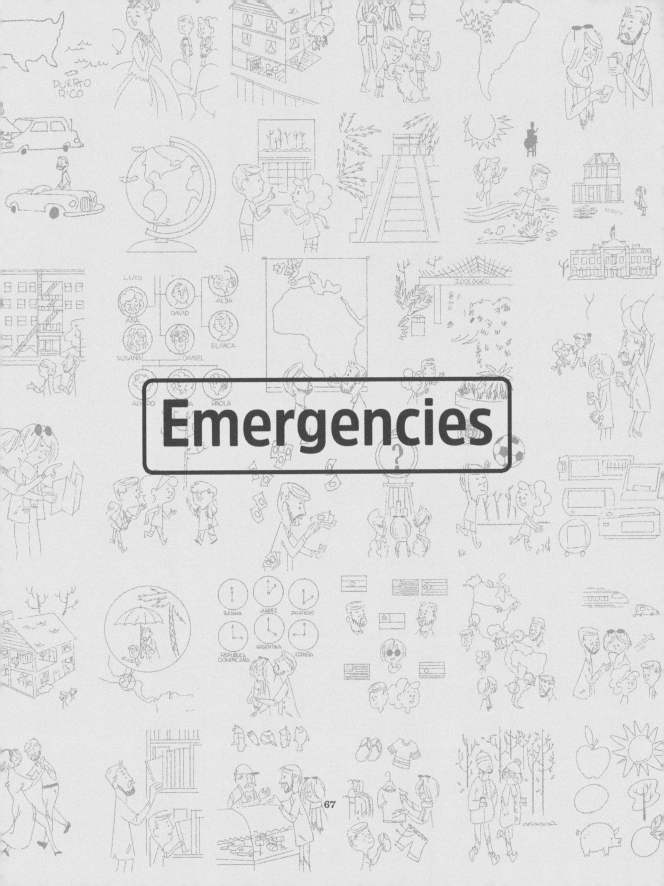

Emergencies

Help Is on the Way!

> **REMEMBER**
> Conjugations for *-ar*, *-er*, and *-ir* verbs are found in Regular Verb Conjugations on page 185.

Key Terms and Phrases

ayudar	to help
necesitar un médico	to need a doctor
Aquí viene una ambulancia.	Here comes an ambulance.
Marca 911.	Call 911 (informal).
¿Qué pasa?	What's the matter?

Conversation

MATEO Ayúdame, por favor.

MARÍA ¿Qué pasa?

MATEO El hombre está mal. Necesita un médico. Marca 911.

MARÍA OK. Aquí viene una ambulancia.

> **NOTES**
> In Spanish, both *médico* and *doctor* mean *doctor*.
>   911 is used in Mexico, parts of Central America, and parts of South America for emergencies. Before traveling outside the United States, check the emergency numbers of your destination country.

Questions

1. What does María ask Mateo?
2. What does the man on the ground need?
3. What does Mateo ask María to do?
4. What is wrong with the man on the ground?

Answers: 1. ¿Qué pasa? **2.** un médico **3.** Marca 911. **4.** El hombre está mal.

Lost!

Key Terms and Phrases

Disculpe	Excuse me (formal)
¿En qué le puedo ayudar?	How may I help you (formal)?
¿Me puede decir?	Can you tell me?
¡Cómo no!	Of course!
Siga derecho	Go straight (formal)
la cuadra	block
Tome la izquierda	Turn left (formal)
Tome la derecha	Turn right (formal)
Con placer	It's a pleasure

Conversation

MARÍA Disculpe, por favor.

MUJER ¿En qué le puedo ayudar?

MARÍA ¿Me puede decir dónde está la escuela?

MUJER ¡Cómo no! Siga derecho por dos cuadras y tome la izquierda.

MARÍA Tomo la derecha en dos cuadras.

MUJER No, tome la izquierda.

MARÍA Gracias.

MUJER Con placer.

NOTES

You may hear *voltee*, *doble*, or *gire* for *turn*. You may also hear *coja* for *turn* in some countries, but be careful because *coger* (*to take*) is an obscene verb in certain countries.

Directo or *recto* is sometimes also used for *straight ahead*.

La manzana or *el bloque* may also be used for *block*.

Questions

1. What does María say to get the woman's attention?
2. What is María trying to find?
3. What is the first step of directions the woman gives María?
4. What does the woman say to María about turning right or left?

Answers: 1. Disculpe, por favor.   2. la escuela   3. Siga derecho por dos cuadras.   4. Tome la izquierda.

Where's the Restroom?!

Key Terms and Phrases

el mesero/ la mesera	server
¿Dónde está el baño?	Where is the bathroom/restroom?
Está fuera de servicio.	It's out of service.
Está al lado del cajero.	It's next to the cashier.
Por favor no tire el papel higiénico.	Please don't flush the toilet paper.

Conversation

PACO Disculpe, ¿dónde está el baño?

MESERO Está al lado del cajero.

PACO ¿Está fuera de servicio?

MESERO El baño está en servicio.

PACO Me alegro.

MESERO Por favor no tire el papel higiénico.

PACO OK, gracias.

NOTES

In Spain, the term *aseos* is often used to mean *restroom*. In some other countries, you may hear *servicios* when referring to the bathroom.

In some parts of Latin America, it is common to see a sign in the bathroom or have a person tell you *not* to flush the toilet paper but instead put it in the trash can.

Questions

1. Where is the restroom?

2. What does the server say if the toilet is working?

3. What does Paco say when he learns the toilet is working?

4. What does the server request Paco not do in the restroom?

Answers: 1. Está al lado del cajero. 2. El baño está en servicio. 3. Me alegro. 4. Por favor no tire el papel higiénico.

Please Pull Over!

Key Terms and Phrases

la policía	police
¿Sabe por qué lo detuve?	Do you know why I stopped you (formal)?
manejar sobre el límite de velocidad	to drive over the speed limit
pagar una multa	to pay a fine
las placas expiradas	expired licence plates
la licencia de conducir	driver's license
el seguro de auto	car insurance
No lo sabía.	I didn't know.
la siguiente vez	the next time

Conversation

POLICÍA Buenos días. ¿Sabe por qué lo detuve?

MATEO No, señor. ¿Estoy manejando sobre el límite de velocidad?

POLICÍA No.

MATEO Me alegro. No quiero pagar una multa.

POLICÍA El problema es que sus placas están expiradas.

MATEO No lo sabía.

POLICÍA ¿Me puede dar su licencia de conducir y su seguro de auto?

MATEO Sí, aquí están.

POLICÍA Gracias. OK, la siguiente vez tendrá una multa.

> **NOTES**
>
> *Conducir* is also used for *to drive*.

Questions

1. What does the police officer first say to Mateo?

2. Why does Mateo think he got pulled over?

3. What is the real reason Mateo got pulled over?

Answers: 1. ¿Sabe por qué lo detuve?   **2.** Por manejar sobre el límite de velocidad   **3.** Sus placas están expiradas.

I Need a Mechanic

Key Terms and Phrases

el mecánico	mechanic
Mi carro no está funcionando bien.	My car isn't working well.
¿Cuál es el problema?	What's the problem?
Hace un ruido extraño a veces.	It makes a strange sound sometimes.
revisar	to check
el aceite	oil
las llantas	tires
los frenos	brakes
el motor	engine

Conversation

MARÍA Buenas tardes, señor. Mi carro no está funcionando bien.

MECÁNICO ¿Cuál es el problema?

MARÍA Hace un ruido extraño a veces.

MECÁNICO Voy a revisar todo: el aceite, las llantas, los frenos y el motor.

Questions

1. Where does María take her car?

2. What does she tell the mechanic is wrong with her car?

3. What four parts will the mechanic check?

Answers: 1. al mecánico
2. Hace un ruido extraño a veces.
3. el aceite, las llantas, los frenos y el motor

What a Disaster!

REMEMBER

Adjective-noun agreement is very important. You say *Hay un perro* (*There is a dog*) but, if referring to more than one dog, *Hay unos perros* (*There are some dogs*).

Key Terms and Phrases

Hay	There is/There are
¿De veras?	Really?
¡Qué pena! ¡Qué lástima!	What a shame!
Y por . . .	And because of . . .
el terremoto	earthquake
el huracán	hurricane
la inundación	flood
el Caribe	the Caribbean

NOTES

The verb *haber* in this context means *there is* (singular) or *there are* (plural).

Conversation

MARÍA   Mateo, ¡hay un terremoto en Guatemala!

MATEO   ¿De veras? ¡Qué pena! Y por el huracán en el Caribe, hay unas inundaciones en Nicaragua.

MARÍA   ¡Qué lástima!

Questions

1. What's happening in Guatemala?

2. What's happening in the Caribbean?

3. What's happening in Nicaragua?

4. What are two responses when hearing bad news?

Answers: 1. Hay un terremoto.
2. Hay un huracán.   3. Hay unas inundaciones.
4. ¡Qué pena! ¡Qué lástima!

Lessons 40–45

Circle the best term for each sentence.

1. El hombre está enfermo. Necesita (una licencia, un médico, una cuadra).

2. Siga (derecho, ayuda, cajero) y en dos cuadras gire a la derecha.

3. ¿Me puede indicar (placer, dónde, disculpa) está la escuela?

4. El baño está (marque, al lado, fuera) de servicio.

5. Por favor no (tire, sabe, revisa) el papel higiénico.

Correct the **bold** words in the sentences.

6. **El médico** revisa el carro. _____

7. Para llamar la ambulancia, **escribe** 911. _____

8. Para conducir es necesario tener **una multa** de conducir y seguro de auto.

_____

Reply with short answers in Spanish.

9. What is an appropriate reply to hearing bad news? _____

10. What are two verbs that mean *to drive*? _____ _____

Jobs and Careers

It's All in a Day's Work: At School

REMEMBER
Conjugations for -ar, -er, and -ir verbs are found in Regular Verb Conjugations on page 185.

Key Terms and Phrases

el maestro/ la maestra	teacher
los estudiantes	students
la clase	class
enseñar	to teach
la lectura	reading
sacar	to take out
el cuaderno	notebook
las plumas	pens
los lapices	pencils
aprender	to learn

Conversation

MATEO Buenos días, estudiantes. ¿Cómo está la clase hoy?

ESTUDIANTES Bien, gracias, ¿y usted?

MATEO Estoy bien, gracias. Hoy les enseño la lectura.

ESTUDIANTES ¿Qué necesitamos?

MATEO Por favor, saquen sus cuadernos, libros, plumas y lapices.

ESTUDIANTES Nos gusta aprender.

NOTES

Profesor and *profe* also mean *teacher*. Students sometimes address their teacher simply by title (*Maestro, Maestra, Profesor, Profe*).

Bolígrafo is another term for *pen*.

Mateo tells his students *Les enseño* (*I will teach you*), which literally translates to "You all I teach." If he were speaking to just one student, he would say *Te enseño*.

Questions

1. What is Mateo teaching today?

2. What four school supplies do the students need to take out?

3. What do the students like to do?

Answers: 1. la lectura   2. cuadernos, libros, plumas y lápices   3. aprender

It's All in a Day's Work:
At the Hospital

> **REMEMBER**
> Conjugations for *-ar*, *-er*, and *-ir* verbs are found in Regular Verb Conjugations on page 185.

Key Terms and Phrases

todavía	still
enfermo	sick
el enfermero/la enfermera	nurse
tal vez/quizás	maybe/perhaps
la cirugía	surgery
antes que nada	before anything
FIRME estos papeles	sign these papers
el seguro de salud	health insurance
No se preocupe	Don't worry (formal)

Conversation

MARÍA   Paco, todavía está enfermo. Vamos al hospital.

ENFERMERA   Buenos días, soy la enfermera.

PACO   Buenos días. Tal vez necesito una cirugía.

ENFERMERA   Quizás. Antes que nada, por favor firme estos papeles.

PACO   No tengo seguro de salud.

ENFERMERA   No se preocupe.

Questions

1. What two things does María tell Paco?

2. Whom does Paco talk to at the hospital?

3. What does Paco think he might need?

4. What does Paco not have to show the nurse?

Answers: 1. Todavía está enfermo. Vamos al hospital.   2. la enfermera   3. una cirugía   4. seguro de salud

It's All in a Day's Work: At the Restaurant

> **REMEMBER**
> Conjugations for *-ar*, *-er*, and *-ir* verbs are found in Regular
> Verb Conjugations on page 185.

Key Terms and Phrases

Me gustaría una mesa para dos.	I'd like a table for two.
el anfitrión/la anfitriona	host/hostess
pedir	to order
¿Cómo estuvo todo?	How was everything?
Estamos llenos.	We are full.
la cuenta	the bill
¿Acepta tarjetas de crédito?	Do you accept credit cards?

Conversation

MARÍA Buenas tardes, me gustaría una mesa para dos, por favor.

ANFITRIONA Aquí hay menus.

PALOMA ¿Qué va a pedir, María? Voy a pedir la ensalada.

MARÍA Mesera, me gustaría la sopa. A Paloma le gustaría la ensalada.

MESERO ¿Cómo estuvo todo?

PALOMA Muy bien, gracias. Estamos llenos.

MARÍA La cuenta, por favor. ¿Acepta tarjetas de crédito?

MESERO Sí.

Questions

1. What does María ask the hostess?

2. What does Paloma ask María?

3. In the second picture, what does María tell the server?

4. How does María ask for the check?

5. Does the restaurant accept credit cards?

Answers: 1. Me gustaría una mesa para dos. 2. ¿Qué va a pedir? 3. Me gustaría la sopa. A Paloma le gustaría la ensalada. 4. La cuenta, por favor. 5. Sí.

It's All in a Day's Work: Emergency Workers

> **REMEMBER**
> Conjugations for *-ar*, *-er*, and *-ir* verbs are found in Regular
> Verb Conjugations on page 185.

Key Terms and Phrases

el paramédico	paramedic
los bomberos	firefighters
el ladrón/la ladrona	thief
me robó	robbed me
el accidente	accident
el fuego/el incendio	fire (small), fire (big)
estar herido	to be hurt
¡Mira!	Look! (informal)

Conversation

PACO ¡Ladrón!

POLICÍA ¿Qué pasó?

PACO ¡Ese ladrón me robó!

STUART ¡Incendio!

PALOMA Los bomberos llegan.

MATEO ¡Mira! Hay un accidente de carro.

MARÍA ¡Qué pena! La persona está herida.

MATEO El paramédico está con él.

> ### Questions
>
> 1. Who robbed Paco?
>
> 2. Who is going to put out the *incendio*?
>
> 3. Why is the paramedic with the injured person?

Answers: 1. un ladrón 2. los bomberos 3. La persona está herida.

We the People

Key Terms and Phrases

el gobierno	government
el/la presidente/a	president
el/la senador/a	senator
el/la diputado/a	congressman/ congresswoman
votar	to vote
sobre la ley	about the law

Conversation

MATEO Me gusta nuestra senadora, pero no me gusta el diputado.

MARÍA El diputado quiere ser presidente.

MATEO No voy a votar por él.

MARÍA La senadora es muy buena para el gobierno.

MATEO Sí, ella tiene buenas ideas sobre la ley.

Questions

1. Does Mateo like the senator or the congressman?

2. What does *el diputado* want to be?

3. What does María say about the senator?

4. What does Mateo say about the senator?

Answers: 1. la senadora   2. presidente   3. Es muy buena para el gobierno.
4. Ella tiene buenas ideas sobre la ley.

Lesson 46–50

Fill in each blank with the key term that best completes the sentence.

policía	enfermera	pedir	incendio	tarjeta
mesera	bomberos	ladrón	enseña	enfermo
		aprender		

1. El maestro _____ la clase.

2. Usted quiere _____ mucho español.

3. Porque Paco está _____ él habla con la _____.

4. Ella va a _____ la sopa de la _____.

5. El restaurante acepta _____ de crédito.

6. Si un _____ te roba, llama a la _____.

7. Si hay un _____ en la casa, llama a los _____.

8. Name three things in Spanish that may be found in a student's desk.

   _____   _____   _____

9. When you're ready to pay in a restaurant, what (in Spanish) do you ask the server to bring you?_____

Translate the following sentences from English to Spanish.

10. She is hurt. _____

11. We vote for the senator and the president. _____

Everyday Life

What's Going On at School?

Key Terms and Phrases

Estoy aprendiendo.	I'm learning.
¿Estás escuchando?	Are you (informal) listening?
Él está enseñando.	He is teaching.
Estamos leyendo.	We're reading.
Están escribiendo.	They're writing.
las tareas	assignments

Conversation

STUART Estoy aprendiendo español.

PALOMA ¡Qué bueno! ¿Estás escuchando bien al maestro?

STUART Sí. Él está enseñando bien.

MATEO Estudiantes, ¿están escribiendo las tareas?

PALOMA Sí, y estamos leyendo el libro.

MATEO Me alegro.

REMEMBER
You formal (*usted*), he (*él*), she (*ella*), and it all use third-person singular verbs and so are conjugated the same.

NOTES
Expressing the present progressive (something happening right now, e.g., *He is eating*) is similar in Spanish and English. Use the verb *estar* and the present participle of the main verb (the *-ing* form of a verb).

Other terms for *assignments* or *homework* are *deberes*, and *trabajos*. Sometimes the term *escolares* (*school-related*) is used after the words *tareas*, *deberes*, and *trabajos*.

Questions

1. What does Paloma ask Stuart?

2. What does Stuart say about the teacher?

3. What does Mateo ask the two students?

4. How do Stuart and Paloma answer Mateo about what they're doing?

Answers: 1. ¿Estás escuchando al maestro? **2.** Él está enseñando bien. **3.** ¿Están escribiendo las tareas? **4.** Estamos leyendo el libro.

What's Going On at Home?

Key Terms and Phrases

¿Qué hacen?	What are they doing?
Estoy duchándome.	I'm taking a shower.
¿Están usando el baño?	Are you (formal) using the bathroom?
Él está durmiendo.	He is sleeping.
No está haciendo su tarea.	He's not doing his homework.
Ella está mirando televisión.	She's watching TV.
Estamos comiendo.	We're eating.
Están usando sus teléfonos.	They're using their phones.
tampoco	neither/either
mientras	while

Conversation

FRAME 1

PALOMA Mateo, ¿están usando el baño?

MATEO Sí. Estoy duchándome.

FRAME 2

MATEO ¿Qué hacen los niños?

MARÍA Stuart no está haciendo su tarea. Él está durmiendo.

MATEO Paloma no está haciendo su tarea tampoco. Ella está mirando televisión.

FRAME 3

MATEO Estamos comiendo mientras que los niños están usando sus teléfonos.

MARÍA Están haciendo sus tareas en sus teléfonos.

NOTES
Both *ver* (*to see*) and *mirar* (*to watch*) are used to mean *watching TV*.

Questions

1. What does Paloma ask Mateo?

2. How does Mateo respond to Paloma?

3. What does Mateo ask María about the children?

4. What is Stuart doing on the sofa?

5. What is Paloma doing on the chair?

6. What does Mateo tell María about what the two adults are doing?

7. What does María tell Mateo about what the two children are doing?

Answers: 1. ¿Están usando el baño? **2.** Estoy duchándome. **3.** ¿Qué hacen los niños? **4.** Stuart está durmiendo. **5.** Paloma está mirando televisión. **6.** Estamos comiendo. **7.** Están haciendo sus tareas en sus teléfonos.

What's Going On at the Party?

Key Terms and Phrases

todos	everyone
la vida	life
No estoy haciendo nada.	I'm not doing anything.
¿Qué están celebrando?	What are you (plural) celebrating?
Estamos celebrando la vida.	We are celebrating life.
Ellos están bailando y cantando.	They are dancing and singing.
No está hablando mucho.	You (formal) are not talking much.

Conversation

PACO   ¿Qué hacen todos?

MARÍA   Stuart y Paloma están bailando y cantando.

PACO   ¿Qué están celebrando?

MARÍA   Todos estamos celebrando la vida. Paco, no está hablando mucho.

PACO   No estoy haciendo nada.

Questions

1. What does Paco ask María?
2. What does María say that Stuart and Paloma are doing?
3. What does María say they are celebrating?
4. Is Paco talking a lot?
5. What is Paco doing?

Answers: 1. ¿Qué hacen todos?   2. Stuart y Paloma están bailando y cantando.   3. la vida   4. No está hablando mucho.   5. No está haciendo nada.

Let's Go to the Pool

Key Terms and Phrases

la piscina	the pool
El salvavidas es simpático.	The lifeguard is nice.
¿Te gusta nadar?	Do you (informal) like to swim?
Me encanta nadar.	I love to swim.
No sé nadar muy bien.	I don't know how to swim very well.
¡Tengan cuidado!	Be careful! (plural)
No corran.	Don't run. (plural)
El piso está mojado.	The floor is wet.

Conversation

PALOMA ¡Estamos aquí en la piscina!

STUART ¿Te gusta nadar?

PALOMA Me encanta nadar, pero no sé nadar muy bien.

SALVAVIDAS Tengan cuidado. No corran ustedes.

STUART ¿Por qué?

SALVAVIDAS Porque el piso está mojado.

PALOMA El salvavidas es simpático.

Questions

1. What does Paloma first say to Stuart?
2. What does Stuart ask Paloma?
3. Does Paloma like to swim?
4. What two commands does the lifeguard give to Stuart and Paloma?
5. What reason does the lifeguard give for his orders?
6. What does Paloma think of the lifeguard?

Answers: 1. ¡Estamos aquí en la piscina! 2. ¿Te gusta nadar? 3. Le encanta nadar. 4. Tengan cuidado. No corran ustedes. 5. Porque el piso está mojado. 6. El salvavidas es simpático.

My Condolences

Key Terms and Phrases

Mis sentidas condolencias	My deep condolences
La muerte de un padre es difícil.	The death of a parent is difficult.
Siento mucho su pérdida.	I'm very sorry for your loss.
Él falleció en paz.	He passed away in peace.
El funeral es en la iglesia.	The funeral is at the church.
Es verdad.	It is true.

Conversation

PACO   Mis sentidas condolencias, María.

MARÍA   Gracias.

PACO   Siento mucho su pérdida. La muerte de un padre es difícil.

MARÍA   Es verdad. Pero él falleció en paz.

PACO   ¿Dónde es el funeral?

MARÍA   El funeral es en la iglesia.

Questions

1. What does Paco say to first offer his condolences?

2. How does Paco say *I'm very sorry for your loss*?

3. What does María say about how her father passed away?

4. What does Paco ask María?

5. How does María answer Paco's question?

Answers: 1. Mis sentidas condolencias.   **2.** Siento mucho su pérdida.   **3.** Él falleció en paz.   **4.** ¿Dónde es el funeral?   **5.** El funeral es en la iglesia.

Lessons 51–55

Fill in each blank with the correct conjugation of *estar*.

1. Anna y Patricio _____ enseñando.

2. Itzel _____ aprendiendo.

3. ¿Tú _____ escuchando?

4. Daniel y yo _____ leyendo.

5. Yo _____ escribiendo.

6. What are three possible ways to say *assignments* in Spanish?

   _____   _____   _____

Match the Spanish words and phrases with their English equivalents.

Están usando sus teléfonos.	She's watching TV.
Estoy duchándome.	They're using their phones.
Ella está mirando televisión.	We're eating.
Estamos comiendo.	I'm taking a shower.

Complete the sentence with the best term.

7. ¿Estás _____ el baño?

8. Ella no está bailando, y él no está bailando _____ .

9. ¿_____ están celebrando todos?

CONTINUED

Unscramble the Spanish terms and then write the English translation.

piscina	iglesia	nadar	mojado

10. dnara _____ _____

11. icsanpi _____ _____

12. jamood _____ _____

13. giaiels _____ _____

14. What is an appropriate response when someone tells you that a loved one passed away?

_____

My House Is Your House

REMEMBER
The verb *ser* is used to talk about what
something is in a more permanent state (like
rooms of a house).

Key Terms and Phrases

Bienvenidos a mi casa.	Welcome to my house.
Su casa es muy bonita.	Your (formal) house is very beautiful.
Esta es la sala.	This is the living room.
Esta es la cocina.	This is the kitchen.
Este es el comedor.	This is the dining room.
Este es el baño.	This is the bathroom.
Siéntese.	Have a seat. (singular formal)

NOTES
Esta is for feminine nouns.
　Este is for masculine nouns.
　Some Spanish speakers use the terms
sala de estar, *salón*, or *living* to mean
living room.
　Variations of *have a seat* are *siéntate*
(informal singular), *siéntense* (plural), and
tomar asiento.

CONTINUED

Conversation

MATEO　¡Bienvenidos a mi casa!

PACO　Gracias. Su casa es muy bonita.

MATEO　Gracias. Esta es la sala, esta es la
cocina, este es el comedor, y este es
el baño.

PACO　Me gusta mucho su casa.

MATEO　Gracias. Siéntese, Paco.

PACO　Gracias.

Questions

1. What does Mateo say to welcome Paco to his house?

2. What two comments does Paco make to compliment Mateo's house?

3. In which room does Mateo cook?

4. In which room does Mateo watch TV?

5. In which room does Mateo eat with his family?

6. In which room does Mateo shower?

7. How does Mateo offer Paco a seat?

Answers: 1. Bienvenidos a mi casa.   **2.** Su casa es muy bonita and Me gusta mucho su casa.
3. la cocina   **4.** la sala   **5.** el comedor   **6.** el baño   **7.** Siéntese.

Welcome to More Rooms in My House

Key Terms and Phrases

Este es el cuarto.	This is the bedroom.
Este es el sótano.	This is the basement.
Este es el jardín.	This is the yard/garden.
Este es el patio.	This is the patio.
Esta es la oficina.	This is the office.
Qué lindos.	How cute.

Conversation

MATEO   Paco, este es el cuarto.

PACO   Me gusta.

MATEO   Este es el jardín y el patio.

PACO   Qué bonitos.

MATEO   Este es el sótano y la oficina.

PACO   Qué lindos.

> **NOTES**
> Some Spanish speakers use the terms *la habitación*, *el dormitorio,* or *la recámara* to express *bedroom*.

Questions

1. What three comments does Paco make to compliment Mateo's house?

2. In which room does Mateo sleep?

3. Where does Mateo sit outside?

4. Where does Mateo's grass grow?

5. In which part of the house is Mateo's office?

Answers: 1. Me gusta, Qué bonitos, and Qué lindos   2. el cuarto   3. el patio   4. el jardín   5. el sótano

Renting an Apartment

Key Terms and Phrases

Estoy buscando un apartamento amueblado.	I'm looking for a furnished apartment.
el/la agente	agent
¿Cuánto es la renta?	How much is the rent?
¿Cuánto puede pagar?	How much can you (formal) pay?
$500 al mes	$500 a month
¿Cuántas habitaciones desea?	How many bedrooms do you (formal) want?
¿Se permiten mascotas?	Are pets allowed?
¿En qué zona está pensando?	Which area are you (formal) thinking about?
Algo cerca del centro de la ciudad	Something close to downtown
Tengo algunos disponibles.	I have some available.

Los servicios están incluidos.	Utilities are included.
Quisiera alquilarlo.	I'd like to rent it.
el depósito	the deposit
¿Cuándo desea mudarse?	When do you (formal) want to move in?
Tan pronto como sea posible	As soon as possible

Conversation

PACO   Estoy buscando un apartamento amueblado. ¿Cuánto es la renta?

AGENTE   ¿Cuánto puede pagar?

PACO $500 al mes.

AGENTE   ¿Cuántas habitaciones desea?

PACO   Una. ¿Se permiten mascotas?

AGENTE   Sí. ¿En qué zona está pensando?

PACO   Algo cerca del centro de la ciudad.

AGENTE   Tengo algunos disponibles, pero los servicios no están incluidos.

PACO   Está bien. Quisiera alquilarlo. ¿Cuánto es el depósito?

AGENTE $500. ¿Cuándo desea mudarse?

PACO   Tan pronto como sea posible.

NOTES

Another term for *the rent* is *el alquiler*.

Another term for *apartment* is *el piso* or *el departamento*.

Another term for *deposit* is *la fianza*.

Questions

1. How much can Paco pay a month for his rent?

2. What does the agent ask him about bedrooms?

3. What does Paco ask about pets?

4. In which area does Paco want to live?

5. What does the agent tell Paco about utilities for the apartments she has to offer?

6. How soon does Paco want to move?

Answers: 1. $500   2. ¿Cuántas habitaciones desea?   3. ¿Se permiten mascotas?   4. Algo cerca del centro de la ciudad.   5. Los servicios no están incluidos.   6. Tan pronto como sea posible.

Lessons 56–58

In which room or area of a house are you most likely to do the following (answer in Spanish)?

1. prepare dinner _____

2. eat dinner _____

3. take a shower _____

4. sleep _____

5. complete assignments on your computer _____

6. go if there is a tornado _____

7. plant flowers _____

8. What is a polite expression in Spanish to say when somebody arrives at your house?

_____

9. What is a polite expression in Spanish to tell somebody that their house is nice?

_____

10. How could you politely ask somebody to have a seat? _____

11. What are three alternate terms for *bedroom*? _____ _____ _____

Translate the following sentences from Spanish to English.

12. ¿Cuánto es la renta? _____

13. ¿Cuántas habitaciones desea? _____

14. Los servicios están incluidos. _____

15. Quisiera alquilarlo. _____

What Are You Going to Do?

Key Terms and Phrases

¿Qué van a hacer hoy?	What are you (plural) going to do today?
Voy a estudiar.	I'm going to study.
Vas a hacer las tareas.	You (informal) are going to do homework.
Va a trabajar.	You are going to work.
Vamos a ir a la escuela.	We are going to go to school.
Van a dar un paseo.	You (formal) are going to take a walk.
Voy a disfrutar.	I'm going to have fun.

Conversation

MATEO ¿Qué van a hacer hoy?

STUART Voy a estudiar. Paloma, ¿vas a hacer las tareas?

PALOMA Sí, y después vamos a ir a la escuela.

MATEO Y usted, Paco, ¿va a trabajar?

PACO No.

MATEO Oh, usted y María van a dar un paseo.

PACO ¡Sí! No voy a trabajar hoy. ¡Voy a disfrutar!

REMEMBER

The conjugation in Spanish is the same for the following subject pronouns: *usted*, *él*, and *ella*. Remember that *él* is used for all masculine nouns, and *ella* is used for all feminine nouns, whether people, animals, or things.

Because Paco is older than Mateo, Mateo uses the formal *usted* with him instead of the informal *tú*.

CONTINUED

NOTES

As in English, one way to express a future action is to use the verb *to go* plus the action verb in its infinitive form (not conjugated). For example, *I am going to eat = Voy a comer.*

In some Spanish-speaking regions, *pasear* is used instead of *dar un paseo* for *take a walk.*

Questions

1. What does Mateo ask everyone?

2. What does Stuart ask Paloma?

3. What does Paloma say that she and Stuart are going to do later?

4. What does Mateo ask Paco?

5. What are Paco and María going to do?

6. Is Paco going to have fun?

Answers: 1. ¿Qué van a hacer hoy? **2.** ¿Vas a hacer las tareas? **3.** Vamos a ir a la escuela. **4.** ¿Va a trabajar? **5.** Van a dar un paseo. **6.** ¡Sí!

Travel

Planes, Trains, and Automobiles!

Key Terms and Phrases

¿Cómo van a viajar?	How are you (plural) going to travel?
en carro	by car (in a car)
en avión	by plane (on a plane)
en tren	by train (on a train)

Conversation

PACO ¿Cómo van a viajar para visitar la familia?

MARÍA Mateo y yo vamos en tren.

STUART Voy en avión.

PALOMA Voy en carro.

Questions

1. What does Paco ask everyone?

2. How does María answer Paco?

3. How does Stuart answer Paco?

4. How does Paloma answer Paco?

Answers: 1. ¿Cómo van a viajar?   **2.** Mateo y yo vamos en tren.   **3.** Voy en avión.   **4.** Voy en carro.

More Than Planes, Trains, and Automobiles!

Key Terms and Phrases

¿Cómo llegan al aeropuerto?	How are you (plural) getting to the airport?
tomar un taxi	to take a taxi
a pie	on foot
en bus	by bus
en barco	by boat

Conversation

PACO ¿Cómo llegan al aeropuerto?

MARÍA Mateo y yo vamos a tomar un taxi.
Después vamos a pie.

STUART Voy en bus. Paloma, ¿vas en barco?

PALOMA No voy en barco. Voy en tren.

> **NOTES**
> Ride-sharing apps are common in Spanish-speaking countries.

Questions

1. What does Paco ask everyone?

2. How does María answer Paco's question?

3. How does Stuart answer Paco?

4. How does Paloma answer Stuart?

Answers: 1. ¿Cómo llegan al aeropuerto? **2.** Mateo y yo vamos a tomar un taxi. Depués vamos a pie. **3.** Voy en bus. **4.** No voy en barco. Voy en tren.

Fly Me Away

Key Terms and Phrases

¿Cómo se llega al aeropuerto?	How do you get to the airport?
El taxista sabe.	The taxi driver knows.
¿Cuál es el número de puerta para el vuelo?	What's the flight's gate number?
¿Tienes tu tarjeta de embarque?	Do you (informal) have your boarding pass?
¿Cuándo sale el vuelo?	When does the flight leave?
¿Cuándo llega el vuelo?	When does the flight arrive?
¿Dónde está el reclamo de equipaje?	Where is the baggage claim?
equipaje de mano	carry-on luggage
maleta	suitcase

Conversation

MARÍA ¿Cómo se llega al aeropuerto?

MATEO El taxista sabe. ¿Cuál es el número de puerta para el vuelo?

MARÍA B-32. ¿Tienes tu tarjeta de embarque?

MATEO Sí. ¿Cuándo sale el vuelo?

MARÍA A las 2:32. ¿Cuándo llega el vuelo?

MATEO A las 5:12. ¿Dónde está el reclamo de equipaje?

MARÍA No lo sé. No tengo maleta. Sólo tengo equipaje de mano.

NOTES

Another term for *boarding pass* is *el pase de abordar*.

Questions

1. What is the flight's gate number?

2. Does Mateo have his boarding pass?

3. What time does the flight leave?

4. What time does the flight arrive?

5. How does María answer Mateo about checked luggage?

Answers: 1. B-32   2. Sí.   3. a las 2:32   4. a las 5:12   5. No tengo maleta. Tengo equipaje de mano.

All Aboard!

Key Terms and Phrases

¿Esta es la estación de trenes?	Is this the train station?
¿Cómo le puedo ayudar?	How may I help you (formal)?
¿Dónde puedo comprar billetes de tren?	Where can I buy train tickets?
¿A dónde va?	Where are you going (formal)?
directo	direct
un billete de ida	one-way ticket
un billete de ida y vuelta	round-trip ticket
el horario	schedule
¿En qué parada me bajo?	At what stop do I get off?

Conversation

PACO Disculpe, ¿esta es la estación de trenes?

AGENTE Sí. ¿Cómo le puedo ayudar?

PACO ¿Dónde puedo comprar billetes de tren?

AGENTE Aquí. ¿A dónde va?

PACO Voy a San Juan.

AGENTE ¿Le gustaría un billete de ida o un billete de ida y vuelta?

PACO De ida y vuelta, por favor. ¿Tiene usted el horario?

AGENTE Sí. Y el tren es directo.

NOTES

The term *ferrocarril* is sometimes used for *railway*.

Questions

1. Where is Paco?

2. Where does Paco want to go by train?

3. What type of ticket does Paco want to purchase?

4. Does the agent give Paco a train schedule?

Answers: 1. Paco está en la estación de trenes.   2. a San Juan   3. un billete de ida y vuelta   4. Sí.

At the Bus Station

Key Terms and Phrases

¿Esta es la estación de autobuses?	Is this the bus station?
¿Cuánto cuesta un boleto a Asunción?	How much is a ticket to Asunción?
Debe comprar el boleto antes de subir al bus.	You (formal) should buy your ticket before getting on the bus.
¿Cuántas horas dura el viaje?	How long is the trip?

Conversation

MATEO ¿Esta es la estación de autobuses?

AGENTE Sí. ¿Cómo le puedo ayudar?

MATEO ¿Cuánto cuesta un boleto a Asunción?

AGENTE 100,000 guaraníes. Debe comprar el boleto antes de subir al bus.

MATEO Muy bien. Me gustaría comprar un boleto a Asunción. ¿Cuántas horas dura el viaje?

AGENTE Tres horas.

Questions

1. Where is Mateo?
2. Where does Mateo want to go by bus?
3. How much does a bus ticket cost to get there?
4. What advice does the agent give Mateo?
5. How long is the trip?

Answers: 1. Mateo está en la estación de autobuses. **2.** a Asunción **3.** 100,000 guaraníes **4.** Debe comprar el boleto antes de subir al bus. **5.** tres horas

NOTES

The terms *boleto* and *billete* are both used to mean *ticket*.

Autobús and *bus* are both used for *bus*.
The currency of Paraguay is the *guaraní*.

Renting a Car

Key Terms and Phrases

¿Dónde se puede alquilar un carro?	Where can you rent a car?
¿Qué tipo de carro le gustaría?	What type of car would you (formal) like?
Algo económico y pequeño.	Something economical and small.
¿Cuánto cuesta por día?	What does it cost per day?
¿Cuánto cuesta por semana?	What does it cost per week?
¿Cuánto cuesta el seguro?	How much is the insurance?
El precio incluye el kilometraje ilimitado.	The price includes unlimited mileage.
¿El auto es estándar o automático?	Is the car manual (stick-shift) or automatic?

NOTES
Spanish-speaking countries use several different currencies; the *peso* is one example.

REMEMBER
The terms *coche*, *auto*, and *carro* are all used to mean *car*.

CONTINUED

Conversation

MARÍA   ¿Dónde se puede alquilar un carro?

AGENTE   Aquí. ¿Qué tipo de carro le gustaría?

MARÍA   Algo económico y pequeño. ¿Cuánto cuesta por día?

AGENTE   20,000 pesos por día. Cuesta 100,000 pesos por semana.

MARÍA   ¿Cuánto cuesta el seguro?

AGENTE   15,000 pesos. El precio incluye el kilometraje ilimitado.

MARÍA   ¿El auto es estándar o automático?

AGENTE   Automático.

Questions

1. What does María first ask the agent?

2. What type of car does María want?

3. What does the car rental cost per day and per week?

4. How much is insurance?

5. Does the price include unlimited mileage?

Answers: 1. ¿Dónde se puede alquilar un carro?   2. Algo económico y pequeño.   3. 20,000 pesos por día y 100,000 pesos por semana.   4. 15,000 pesos   5. Sí.

Lessons 59–65

Complete the sentences with the correct conjugation of *ir* to express who is going to do what.

1. Mi amigo Zen y yo _____ a la escuela.

2. Itzel _____ a hacer las tareas.

3. Isaac y Diego _____ a disfrutar.

4. Yo _____ a dar un paseo.

5. ¿Qué _____ a hacer tú?

6. What are two ways to say *ticket* (for travel)? _____ _____

7. What are seven ways to travel from one place to another? _____
   _____ _____ _____
   _____ _____ _____

Match the Spanish phrases with their English equivalents.

¿Tiene su tarjeta de embarque?	Where can I buy . . . ?
¿Cómo van a viajar?	How may I help you?
¿Cuál es el número de puerta para el vuelo?	Do you have your boarding pass?
¿Cómo le puedo ayudar?	Where is baggage claim?
¿Dónde está el reclamo de equipaje?	How are you going to travel?
¿Dónde puedo comprar . . . ?	What's the flight's gate number?

Translate the following sentence from English to Spanish.

8. I'd like to rent an automatic car for one week with insurance, please.

_____

It's a Sign

Key Terms and Phrases

Vamos a la ciudad.	We're going to the city.
Tenemos prisa.	We're in a hurry.
Baja la velocidad.	Slow down. (informal)
Hay una señal de alto adelante.	There's a stop sign ahead.
la velocidad máxima	the speed limit
Es una calle de una vía.	It's a one-way street.
Esa señal me dice que ceda.	That sign is telling me to yield.
el estacionamiento	parking
Puedes estacionar allí.	You (informal) can park there.

Conversation

MARÍA ¡Vamos a la ciudad! Tenemos prisa.

MATEO Baja la velocidad. Hay una señal de alto adelante.

MARÍA La velocidad máxima es 50.

MATEO Después de la señal de alto, es una calle de una vía.

MARÍA Esa señal me dice que ceda.

MATEO Y esa señal dice *Estacionamiento*. Puedes estacionar allí.

Questions

1. What does Mateo tell María about her speed?

2. How do you translate *stop sign* in Spanish?

3. What is the speed limit?

4. What type of street is after the stop sign?

5. How do you translate *yield* into Spanish?

6. What does the sign say for *parking*?

Answers: 1. Baja la velocidad. 2. la señal de alto 3. 50 4. una calle de una vía 5. ceda 6. estacionamiento

Watch the Traffic!

Key Terms and Phrases

¡Hay mucho tráfico!	There's a lot of traffic!
Estás manejando bien.	You (informal) are driving well.
Tengo que parar aquí en el semáforo.	I have to stop at the traffic light.
Hay la cabina de peaje.	There is the tollbooth.
¿Cuánto cuesta el peaje?	How much is the toll?

Conversation

MARÍA   ¡Hay mucho tráfico!

MATEO   Es verdad. Estás manejando bien.

MARÍA   Tengo que parar aquí en el semáforo.

MATEO   Después del semáforo, hay la cabina de peaje.

MARÍA   ¿Cuánto cuesta el peaje?

MATEO   200 pesos.

Questions

1. What does María first say about why she has to stop?

2. What is after the traffic light?

3. How much is the toll?

4. What are three terms for *tollbooth*?

Answers: 1. Tengo que parar aquí en el semáforo.   **2.** Hay la cabina de peaje.   **3.** 200 pesos   **4.** cabina de peaje, caseta de peaje, puesto de peaje

NOTES

In some regions, you may see *caseta de peaje* or *puesto de peaje* or simply *peaje* for *tollbooth*.

In Mexico, *la cuota* is the term for *toll*.

Beach Day!

Key Terms and Phrases

¡Me encanta la playa!	I love the beach!
jugar en la arena	to play in the sand
jugar en las olas	to play in the waves
la toalla	towel
tomar el sol antes de nadar	to sunbathe before swimming
No quieres quemarte.	You (informal) don't want to burn.
el bloqueador	sunscreen

Conversation

PALOMA ¡Me encanta la playa!

STUART Yo también. Me gusta jugar en la arena.

PALOMA Me gusta jugar en las olas. ¿Tienes toalla?

STUART Sí. Voy a tomar el sol antes de nadar.

PALOMA No quieres quemarte. Aquí hay bloqueador.

> **NOTES**
> In some regions, *asolearse* is used for *sunbathe*.

Questions

1. What does Paloma say about the beach?

2. What does Stuart say he likes to play in?

3. What does Paloma say she likes to play in?

4. What does Stuart say he will do before swimming?

5. What does Paloma give to Stuart?

Answers: 1. ¡Me encanta la playa! **2.** la arena **3.** las olas **4.** tomar el sol **5.** bloqueador

Lodging

Key Terms and Phrases

Me gustaría reservar una habitación.	I'd like to reserve a room.
¿Para cuándo?	For when?
¿Para cuántas personas?	For how many people?
con dos camas y un baño privado	with two beds and a private bathroom
El desayuno está incluido.	Breakfast is included.
¿A qué hora puedo registrarme al hotel?	At what time can I check in to the hotel?
¿A qué hora necesito dejar la habitación?	At what time do I need to check out of the room?
las llaves	keys

Conversation

MARÍA Buenos días, me gustaría reservar una habitación.

AGENTE ¿Para cuándo?

MARÍA Para este fin de semana, dos días.

AGENTE ¿Para cuántas personas?

MARÍA Para dos, con dos camas y baño privado.

AGENTE Muy bien. Cuesta $200, y el desayuno está incluido.

MARÍA ¿A qué hora puedo registrarme al hotel? ¿Y a qué hora necesito dejar la habitación?

MATEO Su habitación será lista a las 2:00. Y usted va a dejar la habitación el domingo a las 11:00.

MARÍA Gracias. Necesito dos llaves.

NOTES

Quisiera is another common way to express *I would like*.

   Cuarto is also used for *room*.

Questions

1. What does María first say to the agent?

2. When does María want the room?

3. For how many people is María reserving the room?

4. Is breakfast included?

5. What time can María check in?

6. What time does María need to check out on Sunday?

7. How many keys does María need?

Answers: 1. Me gustaría reservar una habitación. 2. para este fin de semana 3. dos 4. Sí. 5. a las 2:00 6. a las 11:00 7. dos

Lessons 66–69

Translate the following from English to Spanish.

1. Baja la velocidad. _____.

2. una señal de alto _____

3. la velocidad máxima _____

4. una calle de una vía _____

5. estacionamiento _____

6. ¿Cuánto cuesta el peaje? _____

Unscramble the Spanish terms and then write the English translation.

| playa | toalla | tráfico | bloqueador | semáforo |

7. icrtáof _____   _____

8. fáoesomr _____   _____

9. ylapa _____   _____

10. daeolbrouq _____   _____

11. lataol _____   _____

Answer the questions in Spanish.

12. What might be the first thing you say when trying to reserve a hotel room?

_____

13. How do you ask for two beds and a private bathroom?

_____

Don't Know Much About Geography

Key Terms and Phrases

los mapas	maps
preferir	to prefer
las montañas	mountains
las valles	valleys
la costa	coast
el océano	ocean
pensar sobre	to think about
los volcanes	volcanoes
los desiertos	deserts
la selva	jungle

> **NOTES**
> A map is also called *un plano* in Spain. *El mapa* is an example of an irregular noun because it ends in *a* but is still masculine (*el*, not *la*).

Conversation

STUART Me gustan los mapas.

PALOMA A mí también. ¿Qué prefieres, las montañas o la costa?

STUART Prefiero las montañas y sus valles. Y tú, ¿qué prefieres?

PALOMA Prefiero la costa. Me gusta mirar el océano.

STUART Lo mejor es mirar un río al lado de una montaña.

PALOMA ¿Y que piensas sobre los volcanos y desiertos?

STUART Son interesantes también.

PALOMA Un día quisiera ir a la selva.

Questions

1. ¿Qué prefiere Stuart, las montañas o la costa?

2. ¿Por qué Paloma prefiere la costa?

3. ¿Qué es lo mejor para Stuart?

4. ¿Cómo le parecen los volcanes y los desiertos a Stuart?

5. ¿Un día, a dónde quisiera ir Paloma?

Answers: 1. las montañas   2. Porque le gusta mirar el océano.   3. mirar un río al lado de una montaña   4. Son interesantes.   5. a la selva

Where Can I Try Mate?

Key Terms and Phrases

¿Ha probado . . . ?	Have you (formal) tried . . . ?
el mate	beverage made with yerba mate served hot
se toma	one drinks
el tereré	beverage similar to mate served cold
se usa	one uses
la bombilla	metal straw used to drink mate and tereré

Conversation

MATEO   ¿Ha probado el mate, Paco?

PACO   Sí, en Argentina y Uruguay.

MATEO   Se toma también en Paraguay.

PACO   Es verdad. En Paraguay se toma frío y se llama tereré.

MATEO   Tiene razón. Se usa bombilla con las dos.

Questions

1. ¿Dónde probó Paco el mate?

2. ¿En Paraguay qué se toma?

3. ¿Qué se usa para tomarlo?

Answers: 1. en Argentina y Uruguay   **2.** el tereré   **3.** una bombilla

Falling for Iguazú

Key Terms and Phrases

¿Has visto . . . ?	Have you (informal) seen . . . ?
la catarata	waterfall
¿Dónde puedo ver una?	Where can I see one?
más grandes	bigger/biggest/largest
Están en la frontera entre . . .	They are on the border between . . .
¿No se pueden ver desde . . . ?	You can't see them from . . . ?
Están cerca.	They are close.
Hay que cruzar . . .	You need to cross . . .
Desde . . . hasta	from . . . to
Vámonos.	Let's go.

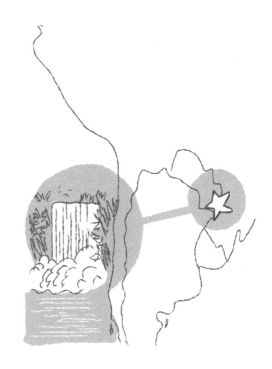

Conversation

MARÍA Paloma, ¿has visto una catarata?

PALOMA No. ¿Dónde puedo ver una?

MARÍA Las cataratas más grandes están en Sudamérica.

PALOMA ¿De veras? ¿Dónde están?

MARÍA Las Cataratas del Iguazú están en la frontera entre Brasil y Argentina.

PALOMA ¿No se pueden ver desde Paraguay?

MARÍA Están cerca, pero hay que cruzar la frontera desde Paraguay hasta Brasil.

PALOMA ¡Vámonos!

CONTINUED

NOTES

Cascada is another term for *waterfall* and is used more in Spain, whereas *catarata* is used more often in Latin America.

Questions

1. ¿Ha visto Paloma una catarata?

2. ¿Dónde están las cataratas más grandes?

3. ¿Las cataratas están en la frontera entre qué países?

4. ¿Están las cataratas cerca de Paraguay?

Answers: 1. No.   2. en Sudamérica   3. Brasil y Argentina   4. Sí.

Tango Time

Key Terms and Phrases

el tango	tango (name of dance)
contigo	with you (informal)
Es popular en otros países.	It's popular in other countries.
Este baile viene de . . .	This dance comes from . . .
los pasos	steps
la música	music

Conversation

MARÍA   Me encanta bailar el tango contigo.

MATEO   Es el baile más popular en Argentina y Uruguay.

MARÍA   ¿De veras? También es popular en otros países.

MATEO   Sí, pero este baile viene de Argentina y Uruguay.

MARÍA   Me gustan los pasos y la música.

Questions

1. ¿Cuál es el baile más popular en Argentina y Uruguay?

2. ¿Este baile es popular en otros países?

3. ¿De dónde viene este baile?

4. ¿Qué le gusta a María?

Answers: 1. el tango   **2.** Sí.   **3.** Argentina y Uruguay   **4.** los pasos y la música

Lessons 70–73

Which land feature is being described?

1. Whales live there. _____

2. The beaches are on it. _____

3. They are between the mountains. _____

4. They erupt. _____

5. It rains a lot there. _____

6. It rarely rains in those places, and there is a lot of sand. _____

7. People ski down these. _____

Translate the following sentences from Spanish to English.

8. ¿Ha probado bailar el tango? _____

9. ¿Has visto las cataratas en Argentina? _____

10. Están en la frontera. _____

11. Vámonos. _____

12. Se toma en Paraguay. _____

Correct the mistakes in the following sentences.

13. Me gustan bailar con tú. _____

14. El tango vienes de Argentina a Uruguay. _____

15. Me gusta el pasos y el música. _____

The Incas

Key Terms and Phrases

Quisiera saber más sobre . . .	I'd like to know more about . . .
el imperio	the empire
América Latina	Latin America
antes de la llegada de Colón	before Columbus's arrival
¿Cuales países actuales fueron parte de . . . ?	Which current countries were part of . . . ?
La capital era . . .	The capital was . . .
¿Qué idioma hablaban?	What language did they speak?
Todavía hay personas que . . .	There are still people who . . .
principalmente	mainly
¿Cuál es la ruina inca más famosa?	What are the most famous Inca ruins?

Conversation

STUART Quisiera saber más sobre los incas.

PACO El Imperio inca fue el más grande de América Latina antes de la llegada de Colón.

STUART ¿De veras? ¿Cuales países actuales fueron parte del imperio?

PACO La capital era Cusco en Perú. También partes de Ecuador, Colombia, Bolivia, Chile y Argentina fueron parte del imperio.

STUART ¿Qué idioma hablaban los incas?

PACO Quechua. Todavía hay personas que hablan Quechua, principalmente en Perú, Ecuador y Bolivia.

STUART ¿Cuál es la ruina inca más famosa?

PACO Machu Picchu.

CONTINUED

Questions

1. ¿De qué quisiera saber más Stuart?

2. ¿El Imperio inca fue el más grande de Norteamérica o de América Latina?

3. ¿Cuales países actuales fueron parte del imperio?

4. ¿Dónde era la capital?

5. ¿Qué idioma hablaban los incas?

6. ¿Todavía hay personas que hablan el idioma de los incas?

7. ¿Cuál es la ruina inca más famosa?

Answers: 1. de los incas   **2.** América Latina   **3.** partes de Perú, Ecuador, Colombia, Bolivia, Chile y Argentina   **4.** Cusco, Perú   **5.** Quechua   **6.** Sí.   **7.** Machu Picchu

Let's Go to the Equator!

Key Terms and Phrases

el ecuador	equator
En Sudamérica se puede visitar . . .	In South America you can visit . . .
significar	to mean

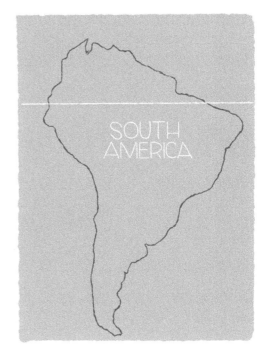

SOUTH AMERICA

Conversation

PALOMA Me gustaría viajar al ecuador.

PACO Yo también. En Sudamérica se puede visitar el ecuador en Ecuador, Colombia y Brasil.

PALOMA El país Ecuador significa el ecuador.

PACO Sí, tienes razón.

PALOMA ¿Hace mucho calor en el ecuador?

PACO Depende si estás en las montañas o en la costa. Hace calor en la costa.

Questions

1. ¿A dónde les gustaría viajar a Paloma y Paco?

2. ¿Por cuáles países de Sudamérica pasa el ecuador?

3. ¿En qué parte del ecuador hace calor, en las montañas o en la costa?

Answers: 1. al ecuador   2. Ecuador, Colombia y Brasil   3. en la costa

Climbing the Andes

Key Terms and Phrases

los Andes	the Andes
la cordillera más larga del mundo	the longest mountain range in the world
¿Qué más hay?	What else is there?
los glaciares	glaciers
los lagos	lakes
los bosques	forests
el volcán más alto del mundo	the tallest volcano in the world

Conversation

STUART Me gustan las montañas. Me gustaría saber más de las montañas en Sudamérica.

MATEO Los Andes son la cordillera más larga del mundo.

STUART ¿Qué países tienen los Andes?

MATEO Venezuela, Colombia, Ecuador, Perú, Bolivia, Argentina y Chile.

STUART ¿Qué más hay en estas montañas?

MATEO Hay glaciares, volcanes, desiertos, lagos y bosques.

STUART ¿Dónde está el volcán más alto del mundo?

MATEO ¡En Ecuador, en la cordillera de los Andes!

Questions

1. ¿Como se llama la cordillera más larga del mundo?

2. ¿Qué países tienen los Andes?

3. ¿Hay desiertos en los Andes?

4. ¿Dónde está el volcán más alto del mundo?

Answers: 1. los Andes   2. Venezuela, Colombia, Ecuador, Perú, Bolivia, Argentina y Chile   3. Sí.   4. en Ecuador, en la cordillera de los Andes

Let's Visit Some Pyramids

Key Terms and Phrases

¿Sabías que hay pirámides en países donde se habla español?	Did you (informal) know there are pyramids in countries where Spanish is spoken?
fueron construidos	were built
antes del siglo 16	before the 16th century

Conversation

STUART ¿Sabías que hay pirámides en países donde se habla español?

PALOMA ¿En qué países?

STUART En México, Guatemala, El Salvador y Honduras.

PALOMA ¡Qué interesante!

STUART ¿Verdad? También hay pirámides en Perú.

PALOMA Las pirámides fueron construidas antes de la llegada de Colón.

STUART Sí, antes del siglo 16.

Questions

1. ¿En qué países hay pirámides donde se habla español?
2. ¿Las pirámides fueron construidas antes de la llegada de quién?
3. ¿Cuándo fueron construidas las pirámides?

Answers: 1. México, Guatemala, El Salvador, Honduras y Perú   2. Colón   3. antes del siglo 16

Lessons 74–77

Complete the paragraph with the Spanish terms that make the most sense.

El (1) _____ inca fue el más grande de (2) _____ antes

de la (3) _____ de Colón. La (4) _____ era Cusco en Perú.

(5) _____ partes de Ecuador, Colombia, Bolivia, Chile y Argentina fueron

(6) _____ del imperio. Los incas hablaban el (7) _____

Quechua.

Answer the following questions.

8. ¿Qué significa *ecuador* en ingles? _____

9. ¿Cómo se llaman las montañas en Sudamérica? _____

10. Los Andes son la cordillera más larga del mundo, ¿sí o no? _____

Verdadero o Falso = True or False

Put a *V* for true statements and an *F* for false statements. If a statement is false, correct the statement.

11. Hay glaciares en los Andes. _____

12. Hay bosques en los Andes. _____

13. El volcán mas alto del mundo está en Chile. _____

14. Venezuela, Colombia, Ecuador, Perú, Bolivia, Argentina y Paraguay son los países que tienen los Andes. _____

What About Central America?

Key Terms and Phrases

Centroamérica	Central America
Muchos turistas vienen.	Many tourists come.
conocer	to be familiar with a place
el canal	canal
más cercanos	closest

Conversation

PALOMA Soy de Centroamérica.

MARÍA Eres de Costa Rica, ¿verdad?

PALOMA Sí. Muchos turistas vienen a mi país.

MARÍA ¿Conoces los otros países de Centroamérica?

PALOMA Conozco los países más cercanos, Panamá y Nicaragua.

MARÍA Panamá tiene un canal famoso.

PALOMA Sí. Y Nicaragua es muy bonito.

> **NOTES**
> Central America is also called *América Central.*
>
> *Conocer* means *to know* when referring to people or *to be familiar with* (usually as a result of having visited the country/city) when referring to places.

Questions

1. ¿Paloma es de qué país?

2. ¿Muchos o pocos turistas vienen a su país?

3. ¿Qué países son los más cercanos al país de Paloma?

4. ¿Qué país tiene un canal?

5. ¿Qué país dice Paloma que es muy bonito?

Answers: 1. Costa Rica   2. muchos
3. Panamá y Nicaragua   4. Panamá
5. Nicaragua

What Other Countries Are in Central America?

Key Terms and Phrases

Hay islas.	There are islands.
el Imperio maya	the Mayan Empire
amable	nice/friendly
no se habla	it is not spoken (as in a language)

BELIZE
HONDURAS
GUATEMALA
EL SALVADOR

Conversation

MARÍA ¿Deseas conocer los otros países en Centroamérica?

PALOMA Sí. Hay islas bonitas cerca de Honduras.

MARÍA Y Guatemala tiene muchas ruinas del Imperio maya.

PALOMA Sí. Y las personas de El Salvador son amables.

MARÍA No se habla español en Belice.

PALOMA Hay personas que hablan español en Belice, pero hay más que hablan inglés.

Questions

1. ¿Hay islas bonitas cerca de qué país?
2. ¿Qué tiene Guatemala?
3. ¿Qué dice Paloma de las personas de El Salvador?
4. ¿Se habla inglés en Belice?

Answers: 1. Honduras   2. muchas ruinas del Imperio maya   3. Son amables.   4. Sí.

Lessons 78–79

Complete the paragraph with the Spanish terms that make the most sense.

Hay pirámides en países donde (1) _____ español. Los

(2) _____ donde las hay son México, Guatemala, El Salvador,

Honduras y (3) _____ Perú. Las pirámides fueron construidas

(4) _____ la llegada de Colón, antes del (5) _____ 16.

6. What are two ways to say *Central America*? _____ _____

Verdadero o Falso = True or False

Put a *V* for true statements and an *F* for false statements. If a statement is false, correct the statement.

7. El Salvador tiene un canal famoso. _____

8. Panamá y Nicaragua son los países más cercanos a Costa Rica. _____

9. En Belice se habla más español que inglés. _____

10. Guatemala tiene muchas ruinas del Imperio maya. _____

11. No hay islas bonitas cerca de Honduras. _____

How would you express the following sentence in English?

12. No conozco los países en América Central.

_____

Puerto Rico, Island of Enchantment

Key Terms and Phrases

Estoy muy emocionada	I'm very excited.
Necesita una visa.	You (formal) need a visa.
No es un estado.	It is not a state.
Tengo pasaporte americano.	I have an American passport.
la isla del encanto	the island of charm
con buen clima todo el año	with good weather all year long

Conversation

MARÍA   Estoy muy emocionada de viajar a Puerto Rico.

PACO   Yo también. Porque usted es de Chile, María, necesita una visa para viajar desde los Estados Unidos.

MARÍA   Es verdad. Usted no necesita una visa, Paco, porque Puerto Rico es un territorio de los EEUU y usted es ciudadano americano.

PACO   Sí, soy. Puerto Rico no es un estado de los EEUU, pero tengo pasaporte americano.

MARÍA   ¿Por qué se llama su isla "la isla del encanto"?

PACO   Porque es una isla muy bonita con buen clima todo el año.

NOTES

The abbreviation in Spanish for *Estados Unidos* is *EEUU*, meaning *USA*.

Questions

1. ¿A dónde están viajando Paco y María?
2. ¿Por qué María necesita una visa?
3. ¿Por qué Paco no necesita una visa?
4. ¿Es Puerto Rico un estado de los EEUU?
5. ¿Tiene Paco pasaporte americano?
6. ¿Por qué Puerto Rico se llama "la isla del encanto"?

Answers: 1. Puerto Rico **2.** Porque es de Chile. **3.** Porque es ciudadano americano. **4.** No. **5.** Sí. **6.** Porque es una isla muy bonita con buen clima todo el año.

Caribbean Rhythms

Key Terms and Phrases

Hay mucha música buena del Caribe.	There is a lot of good music from the Caribbean.
¿Dónde se originó la música salsa?	Where did salsa music originate?
¿Qué tipo de música caribeña . . . ?	What type of Caribbean music . . . ?
Mi favorito es el merengue.	My favorite is merengue.

Conversation

MARÍA   Hay mucha música buena del Caribe.

MATEO   Es verdad. Me gusta más la salsa.

MARÍA   ¿Dónde se originó la música salsa?

MATEO   De Cuba. ¿Qué tipo de música caribeña te gusta más?

MARÍA   Mi favorito es el merengue de la República Dominicana.

MATEO   Ese es bueno. Me gusta también el reggaeton de Puerto Rico.

MARÍA   ¡Estas islas tienen muy buena música!

Questions

1. ¿Qué tipo de música le gusta más a Mateo?
2. ¿Qué tipo de música le gusta más a María?
3. ¿De dónde se originó el reggaeton?
4. ¿De dónde se originó el merengue?
5. ¿Son Cuba, Puerto Rico y la República Dominicana islas?

Answers: 1. la salsa   2. el merengue   3. Puerto Rico   4. la República Dominicana   5. Sí.

Spain: Where Spanish Originated

Key Terms and Phrases

No sé mucho de España.	I don't know much about Spain.
Europa	Europe
Nuestro idioma originó allí.	Our language originated there.
Porque los españoles colonizaron una gran parte de las Américas	Because the Spaniards colonized a big part of the Americas.
el castellano	Castilian
el vasco	Basque
el gallego	Galician
el valenciano	Valencian
Es otra palabra para español.	It's another word for Spanish.

Conversation

PALOMA No sé mucho de España.

MATEO España está en Europa. Nuestro idioma originó allí.

PALOMA ¿Por qué se habla español en América Latina?

MATEO Porque los españoles colonizaron gran parte de las Américas.

PALOMA España tiene playas bonitas, ¿verdad?

MATEO Sí, y muchas ciudades famosas también, como Madrid, Barcelona y Sevilla.

PALOMA ¿Se hablan otros idiomas en España?

MATEO Sí. Se habla principalmente castellano, que es otra palabra para español. También se hablan gallego, vasco, valenciano y catalán.

Questions

1. ¿En qué continente está España?

2. ¿Por qué se habla español en América Latina?

3. ¿Qué son tres ciudades famosas en España?

4. ¿Cuál es otra palabra para el español?

5. ¿Se hablan otros idiomas en España?

Answers: 1. Europa   2. Porque los españoles colonizaron gran parte de las Américas.   3. Madrid, Barcelona y Sevilla   4. castellano   5. Sí, se hablan gallego, vasco, valenciano y catalán.

Lessons 80–82

Match the Spanish and English sentences.

Puerto Rico se llama "la isla del encanto".	I have an American passport.
La isla tiene buen clima todo el año.	It is not a state.
Estoy muy emocionada.	The island has good weather all year.
Tengo pasaporte americano.	Puerto Rico is called "The Island of Enchantment."
No es un estado.	I'm very excited.

Answer the following questions in Spanish.

1. ¿Dónde se originó la música salsa? _____

2. ¿De dónde se originó la música merengue? _____

3. ¿De dónde se originó la música reggaeton? _____

Correct the bold words in the following sentences.

4. No **sabo** mucho de España. _____

5. España está en **Centroamérica**. _____

6. **Castillo** es otra palabra para español. _____

7. También se hablan gallego, vasco, valenciano y **Barcelona** en España. _____

8. España tiene **países** famosas, como Madrid, Barcelona y Sevilla. _____

Out and About on the Town

143

Let's Shop for Clothes:
Warm Weather

Key Terms and Phrases

¿Qué vamos a comprar?	What are we going to buy?
ropa nueva para el clima cálido	new clothes for warmer weather
las camisetas	T-shirts
los pantalones cortos	shorts
el traje de baño	swimsuit
las sandalias	sandals
Ya los tengo.	I already have them.

Conversation

STUART ¿Qué vamos a comprar?

MARÍA Necesitas ropa nueva para el clima cálido.

STUART Necesito camisetas y pantalones cortos.

MARÍA ¿No necesitas traje de baño? ¿No necesitas sandalias?

STUART No. Ya los tengo.

NOTES
La playera is another word for *T-shirt*.
   Las chanclas is another word for *sandals*.

Questions

1. ¿Qué van a comprar?
2. ¿Qué necesita Stuart?
3. ¿Qué no necesita Stuart?
4. ¿Cuál es otra palabra para *T-shirt*?

Answers: 1. ropa nueva para el clima cálido 2. camisetas y pantalones cortos 3. el traje de baño o sandalias 4. la playera

Let's Shop for Clothes: Cold Weather

Key Terms and Phrases

el clima frío	cold weather
los pantalones	pants
los suéteres	sweaters
el abrigo	coat
la bufanda	scarf
los guantes	gloves

Conversation

PALOMA ¿Qué vamos a comprar?

MARÍA Necesitas ropa nueva para el clima frío.

PALOMA Necesito suéteres y pantalones.

MARÍA ¿No necesitas un abrigo?

PALOMA No. Ya lo tengo. Pero necesito una bufanda y unos guantes.

Questions

1. ¿Qué van a comprar, Paloma y María?
2. ¿Qué necesita Paloma?
3. ¿Qué no necesita Paloma?

Answers: 1. ropa nueva para el clima frío   2. suéteres, pantalones, una bufanda y unos guantes   3. un abrigo

Lessons 83–84

Circle the term that does not fit with the theme.

1. sandalias, trajes de baño, bufandas, pantalones cortos

2. guantes, playeras, abrigos, suéteres

Answer with the correct Spanish term.

3. What do you wear to go swimming? _____

4. What type of shoe is common to wear in the summer? _____

5. What do you wear on your hands in the winter? _____

6. What do you wear around your neck in the winter? _____

Translate the following sentences from Spanish to English.

7. ¿Qué vamos a comprar? _____

8. Necesito ropa nueva para el clima frío. _____

9. Tienes ropa para el clima cálido. _____

10. Ya tengo un abrigo y pantalones. _____

Let's Go to the Fruit Market

Key Terms and Phrases

el mercado de frutas	fruit market
las manzanas	apples
los plátanos	bananas (or plantains)
las fresas	strawberries
las naranjas	oranges
las uvas	grapes
¿Cuánto cuesta(n)?	How much does it (do they) cost?
A ver.	We will see.

Conversation

PALOMA ¿Qué va a comprar en el mercado de frutas?

PACO Necesito manzanas, plátanos y fresas.

PALOMA ¿No necesita naranjas? ¿No necesita uvas?

PACO No. Ya las tengo.

PALOMA ¿Cuánto cuestan?

PACO A ver.

NOTES

Sometimes the term *banana* is used instead of *plátano*. There are also several varieties of *plátanos*, some of which must be cooked to be edible. (*Maduros*, ripe plantains, are the most common and are served deep fried.)

Questions

1. ¿Qué va a comprar Paco?
2. ¿Qué no necesita Paco?
3. ¿Por qué no las necesita Paco?
4. ¿Qué le dice Paco a Paloma cuando ella dice "¿Cuánto cuestan?"?

Answers: 1. manzanas, plátanos y fresas   2. naranjas o uvas   3. Porque ya las tiene.   4. A ver.

Let's Go to the Vegetable Market

Key Terms and Phrases

el mercado de vegetales	vegetable market
las papas	potatoes
las zanahorias	carrots
las cebollas	onions
la lechuga	lettuce
el maíz	corn
Es un buen precio.	It's a good price.

Conversation

PALOMA ¿Qué va a comprar en el mercado de vegetales?

PACO Necesito papas, zanahorias y cebollas.

PALOMA ¿No necesita lechuga? ¿No necesita maíz?

PACO No me gustan.

PALOMA ¿Cuánto cuestan?

PACO Es un buen precio.

NOTES

Sometimes the term *patata* is used instead of *papa* for *potato*.

Verdura is another term for *vegetable*. In Spain, *verdura* is used almost exclusively.

Questions

1. ¿Qué va a comprar Paco?

2. ¿Qué no le gusta a Paco?

3. ¿Qué le dice Paco a Paloma cuando ella dice "¿Cuánto cuestan?"?

4. ¿Cuál es otra palabra para *papa*?

Answers: 1. papas, zanahorias y cebollas 2. lechuga y maíz 3. Es un buen precio. 4. patata

Let's Go to the Meat Market

Key Terms and Phrases

el carne	meat
el pollo	chicken
el puerco	pork
el pescado	fish
el carnicero/la carnicera	butcher
¿Cómo les puedo ayudar?	How may I help you (plural)?
libras de cada uno	pounds of each
Bienvenidos a mi carnicería.	Welcome to my butcher shop.

Conversation

MATEO   ¿Qué vamos a comprar?

MARÍA   Necesitamos carne, pollo, puerco y pescado.

CARNICERO   Bienvenidos a mi carnicería. ¿Cómo les puedo ayudar?

MATEO   Necesitamos carne y pollo, por favor.

CARNICERO   Está bien. ¿Cuánto?

MATEO   Dos libras de cada uno, por favor.

MARÍA   Y también tres libras de puerco y pescado.

> **NOTES**
> The metric system is mostly used outside the United States, so stating *kilogram* (*kilogramo* in Spanish) instead of *pound* is more common.

Questions

1. ¿Qué van a comprar Mateo y María?
2. ¿Cuánta carne y pollo necesitan?
3. ¿Cuánto puerco y pescado necesitan?
4. ¿Cómo se dice *butcher shop* en español?

Answers: 1. carne, pollo, puerco y pescado
2. dos libras de cada uno   3. tres libras
4. carnicería

How Sweet It Is!

Key Terms and Phrases

la panadería	bakery
el panadero/la panadería	baker
el pan de yuca	yucca bread
el pan de queso	cheese bread
chipá	a cheese bread unique to Paraguay and parts of Argentina
algunos pasteles	some pastries
el churro	similar to a doughnut but cylinder shaped
el pastel de tres leches	cake made with three kinds of milk
el pan dulce	sweet bread
los dólares	dollars

Conversation

PANADERA   Bienvenidos a mi panadería. ¿Cómo te puedo ayudar?

STUART   Buenos días. ¿Qué tipos de pan tiene?

PANADERA   Tenemos pan de yuca, pan de queso y chipá.

STUART   Quisiera pan de yuca, por favor.

PANADERA   Está bien. ¿Te gustaría algunos pasteles también?

STUART   ¡Cómo no! ¿Qué tiene?

PANADERA   Tenemos churros, pasteles de tres leches y pan dulce.

STUART   Quisiera cuatro churros, por favor. ¿Cuánto es?

PANADERA   Sería dos dólares, por favor.

NOTES

The U.S. dollar ($) is the currency in some Latin American countries (e.g., Panama) and is accepted in a few others.

Questions

1. ¿Dónde está Stuart?
2. ¿Qué tipos de pan tiene?
3. ¿Qué tipo de pan quiere Stuart?
4. ¿Qué tipos de pasteles tiene?
5. ¿Qué tipo de pastel quiere Stuart?
6. ¿Cuánto cuestan cuatro churros?

Answers: 1. en la panadería   **2.** pan de yuca, pan de queso y chipá   **3.** pan de yuca   **4.** churros, pasteles de tres leches y pan dulce   **5.** churros   **6.** dos dólares

Lessons 85–88

1. Circle three things you will not find at *el mercado de frutas*.

| uvas | pan | fresas | manzanas | maíz | cebollas |

2. Circle three things you will not find at *el mercado de vegetales*.

| plátanos | naranjas | zanahorias | papas | lechuga | pasteles |

3. Name four types of meat you can find at *la carnicería*.

_____   _____

_____   _____

4. Circle two things you will not find at *la panadería*.

| lechuga | puerco | chipá | pastel de tres leches | pan de yuca | churros |

Correct the bold words in the following sentences.

5. ¿Cuánto **cuestas** una manzana? _____

6. Es **buena** precio. _____

7. ¿Cómo les puedo **ayudo**? _____

8. No me **gusta** las naranjas. _____

9. **¿Dónde** tipos de pan tiene? _____

10. ¿Cuántos **dolor** cuesta? _____

11. What's another term for *papas*? _____

12. What's another term for *vegetales*? _____

Let's Bargain!

Key Terms and Phrases

¡Está cobrando demasiado!	You're (formal) charging too much!
Está hecho a mano	It's made by hand.
¿Cuál es su mejor precio?	What's your (formal) best price?
Le doy . . .	I'll give you (formal) . . .
el vendedor/la vendedora	vendor
el collar	necklace

Conversation

MARÍA   Buenos días. ¿Cuánto cuesta esto?

VENDEDOR   Diez dólares.

MARÍA   ¡Está cobrando demasiado!

VENDEDOR   No, señora, es un buen precio. Está hecho a mano.

MARÍA   Es bonito. ¿Cuál es su mejor precio?

VENDEDOR   Nueve dólares.

MARÍA   Le doy siete dólares.

VENDEDOR   Acepto ocho dólares.

MARÍA   OK, está bien.

> **NOTES**
> Bargaining, or negotiating the price, is common with and expected by vendors in certain establishments in Latin America, especially the outdoor markets.
>
> It is also common to hear *¿Qué precio tiene?* when inquiring about the cost of something.

Questions

1. ¿Cuánto cuesta el collar?

2. ¿Qué dice María del precio?

3. ¿Por qué el vendedor dice que es un buen precio?

4. How does María ask for the best price?

5. ¿Cuál precio acepta el vendedor?

Answers: 1. diez dólares   2. ¡Está cobrando demasiado!   3. Está hecho a mano.
4. ¿Cuál es su mejor precio?   5. ocho dólares

What's Showing?

Key Terms and Phrases

¡Vamos a ver una película!	Let's go see a movie!
¿Qué películas están exhibiendo en el cine?	What movies are showing at the movie theater?
aventura	adventure
acción	action
animación	animation
ciencia ficción	science fiction
¿De qué se trata?	What's it about?
empezar	to start
terminar	to end
durar	to last
la entrada	ticket
¿Es apropiado para niños?	Is it appropriate for children?

Conversation

STUART ¡Vamos a ver una película!

PALOMA ¿Qué películas están exhibiendo en el cine?

PACO De aventura, de acción, de animación y de ciencia ficción.

STUART Yo quiero ver una de acción.

PACO ¿La película de acción es apropiada para niños?

STUART Mis padres dicen que sí.

PALOMA ¿De qué se trata?

STUART No lo sé.

PALOMA Está bien conmigo. ¿A qué hora empieza la película?

PACO A la 1:30, y termina a las 3:00. Dura una hora y media. Compro las entradas.

NOTES

¿Cuáles películas se presentan en el cine? is also used to ask *What movies are showing at the movie theater?*

Another term for *ticket* is *el boleto*.

Questions

1. ¿Qué películas están exhibiendo en el cine?

2. ¿Qué película quiere ver Stuart?

3. ¿La película es apropriada para niños?

4. ¿A qué hora empieza la película?

5. ¿Cuántas horas dura?

Answers: 1. de aventura, de acción, de animación y de ciencia ficción   2. una de acción   3. Sí.   4. a la 1:30   5. una hora y media

Play Ball!

Key Terms and Phrases

el fútbol	soccer
el fútbol americano	football
el béisbol	baseball
el baloncesto	basketball
el rugby	rugby
la pelota	ball
el equipo	team
el juego	game
el deporte	sport

Conversation

MATEO ¿Qué quieres jugar, Stuart? Tenemos pelotas de fútbol, rugby y béisbol.

STUART El béisbol es mi deporte favorito. ¿Cuál es su deporte favorito?

MATEO Me encanta jugar rugby, pero el fútbol es el deporte más popular del mundo.

STUART Hay muchos buenos equipos de fútbol en países donde se habla español.

MATEO Sí, y también el béisbol es popular en países del Caribe.

STUART ¿Dónde es popular el rugby?

MATEO En América Latina, es popular en Argentina, Paraguay, Uruguay y Chile.

STUART El baloncesto no es muy popular en América Latina.

MATEO Es verdad. El fútbol americano tampoco es popular.

STUART ¡Vamos a jugar un juego!

NOTES

Another term for *basketball* is *básquetbol*.

Questions

1. ¿Cuál es el deporte favorito de Stuart?

2. ¿Cuál es el deporte favorito de Mateo?

3. ¿Cuál es el deporte más popular en América Latina?

4. ¿Dónde es popular el béisbol?

5. ¿Dónde es popular el rugby?

6. ¿Son el baloncesto y el fútbol americano populares en América Latina?

Answers: 1. el béisbol   **2.** el rugby   **3.** el fútbol   **4.** el Caribe   **5.** Argentina, Paraguay, Uruguay y Chile   **6.** No.

What Other Sports?

Key Terms and Phrases

patinar	to skate
los patines	skates
esquiar	to ski
los esquís	skis
el tenis	tennis
la raqueta	racquet
Voy a comprarla para ti.	I'm going to buy it for you (informal).

Conversation

MARÍA   ¿Qué quieres jugar, Paloma?

PALOMA Me gusta patinar, jugar tenis y esquiar.

MARÍA   ¿Tienes patines?

PALOMA Sí. Tengo esquís también.

MARÍA   Me gustaría jugar tenis. ¿Tienes raqueta?

PALOMA No la tengo.

MARÍA   Voy a comprarla para ti.

PALOMA ¡Gracias! Vamos a jugar tenis.

Questions

1. ¿Qué quiere jugar Paloma?
2. ¿Tiene Paloma patines?
3. ¿Tiene Paloma esquís?
4. ¿Qué quiere jugar María?
5. ¿Paloma tiene raqueta?
6. ¿Qué va a comprar María para Paloma?
7. ¿Qué van a jugar Paloma y María?

Answers: 1. patinar, jugar tenis y esquiar   2. Sí.   3. Sí.   4. tenis   5. No.   6. una raqueta   7. tenis

Lessons 89–92

Match each Spanish sentence with its English equivalent.

Está hecho a mano.	You charge too much.
¿Cuál es su mejor precio?	I'll give you five.
Cobra demasiado.	What's your best price?
Le doy cinco.	It's made by hand.

Complete the paragraph with the Spanish terms that make the most sense.

Están exhibiendo muchas películas en (**1**) _____. La película de ciencia

ficción (**2**) _____ del futuro y espacio. La película (**3**) _____

a la 1:30 y (**4**) _____ a las 3:00. Vamos a comprar dos (**5**) _____

y cuestan $11 cada una.

Unscramble the Spanish terms and then write the English translation.

béisbol	equipo	deporte	juego	pelota

6. olatpe   _____   _____

7. oereptd   _____   _____

8. peoqiu   _____   _____

9. sobébli   _____   _____

10. oeguj   _____   _____

CONTINUED

Translate the following sentences from English to Spanish.

11. He loves to play soccer. _____

12. Basketball is his favorite sport. _____

13. They are going to ski. _____

14. I like to skate. _____

A Good Read

Key Terms and Phrases

la biblioteca	library
libros de . . .	books about . . .
misterio	mystery
no ficción	nonfiction
ficción	fiction
la librería	bookstore
Si lo tienen.	If they have it.

Conversation

PACO   Me gusta la biblioteca.

STUART   ¿Qué tipo de libro le gusta, Paco?

PACO   Me gustan los libros de misterio y no ficción. ¿Y tú, Stuart?

STUART   A mi me gustan los libros de aventura. ¿Va a sacar un libro, Paco?

PACO   Si lo tienen. Vamos a la librería para comprar un libro de aventura para ti, Stuart.

> **NOTES**
> *Pedir prestado* is another way to say *check out a book*.

Questions

1. ¿Dónde están Stuart y Paco?
2. ¿Qué tipo de libro le gusta a Paco?
3. ¿Qué tipo de libro le gusta a Stuart?
4. ¿Paco va a sacar un libro?
5. ¿A dónde van para comprar un libro de aventura para Stuart?

Answers: 1. la biblioteca   2. los libros de misterio y no ficción   3. los libros de aventura 4. Si lo tienen.   5. la librería

May I Take Your Order?

Key Terms and Phrases

el restaurante	restaurant
el mesero/la mesera	server
¿Están listas para pedir?	Are you ready to order?
¿Qué me recomienda?	What do you recommend?
por supuesto	of course
Tráigame	Bring me
para tomar	to drink
el tenedor	fork
la cuchara	spoon
el cuchillo	knife
los cubiertos	eating utensils
la servilleta	napkin
el efectivo	cash
el jugo	juice
el agua	water
con hielo	with ice
sin hielo	without ice

los mariscos	seafood
los camarones	shrimp
a la plancha	grilled
asado	roasted
apanado	breaded
a la parrilla	barbecued
delicioso	delicious
la sopa	soup
invitar	to invite

Conversation

MESERA Buenas noches. ¿Están listas para pedir?

MARÍA Sí, quisiera mariscos. ¿Qué me recomienda?

MESERA Los camarones a la plancha son deliciosos.

MARÍA ¿Es mejor que asado, apanado o a la parrilla?

MESERA Creo que sí.

MARÍA OK. Y para tomar, una agua.

MESERA ¿Con hielo o sin hielo?

MARÍA Sin hielo. Y tráigame los cubiertos, por favor. Necesito tenedor, cuchara y cuchillo.

MESERA Por supuesto. ¿Y para ti?

PALOMA Quisiera un jugo de naranja y una sopa, por favor. ¿Puedo pagar en efectivo?

MESERA Por supuesto.

MARÍA Paloma, no vas a pagar.

PALOMA Sí, quiero invitarle, María.

MARÍA ¡Muchas gracias!

NOTES

Ordenar may be used for *to order*.

In Spain, *camarero/a* is the term for *server*.

Invitar in Spanish means that the person who suggested the activity will pay for the person who was invited, similar to "it's on me," in English.

Questions

1. ¿Dónde están María y Paloma?
2. ¿Qué recomienda la mesera a María?
3. ¿María quisiera su agua con hielo o sin hielo?
4. ¿Qué cubiertos necesita María?
5. ¿Qué tipo de jugo quisiera Paloma?
6. ¿Quien va a pagar?
7. ¿Cómo va a pagar?

Answers: 1. el restaurante   2. los camarones a la plancha   3. sin hielo   4. tenedor, cuchara y cuchillo   5. de naranja   6. Paloma   7. en efectivo

I Need a Haircut

Key Terms and Phrases

el salón de belleza	beauty salon/hair salon
lavar	to wash
el cabello	hair (as in "head of hair")
el champú	shampoo
el acondicionador	conditioner
cortarse el pelo	to get a haircut
las puntas	ends
cortar las puntas	to trim (hair)
el/la estilista	hairstylist
Antes que nada me pongo . . .	Before anything else, I put on . . .

NOTES

La peluquería is another term for *hair salon*.

Cabello refers to hair on one's head.

Pelo is *hair* as in a strand or piece.

Conversation

EL ESTILISTA   Buenos días. ¿Qué le gustaría hacer hoy?

MARÍA   Por favor, lava y corta mi cabello.

EL ESTILISTA   Muy bien. ¿Voy a cortar mucho o poco?

MARÍA   Quiero que sólo me corte las puntas.

EL ESTILISTA   OK. Antes que nada, pongo el champú y el acondicionador.

MARÍA   Gracias.

Questions

1. ¿Dónde está María?

2. ¿Cómo se dice en español *Wash and cut my hair*?

3. ¿María quiere que el estilista corte mucho o poco?

4. How does María tell the stylist that she just wants him to trim the ends?

5. What does the stylist say he'll put on first?

6. What is the difference between *cabello* and *pelo*?

Answers: 1. el salón de belleza **2.** Lave y corte mi cabello. **3.** poco **4.** Quiero que sólo me corte las puntas. **5.** el champú y el acondicionador **6.** *Cabello* is a head of hair, and *pelo* is an individual piece or strand of hair.

At the Zoo

Key Terms and Phrases

el zoológico	zoo
¿Qué animales te gusta ver?	What animals do you (informal) like to see?
los monos	monkeys
las jirafas	giraffes
los elefantes	elephants
los pájaros/ los aves	birds
chistoso	funny
tan	so
Hay mucha variedad.	There's a lot of variety.

> **NOTES**
>
> *Pájaros* and *aves* both mean *birds*. *Pájaro* generally refers to a small bird that flies, whereas *ave* refers to the bird species as well as larger birds and flightless birds.

Conversations

PALOMA ¡Me encanta el zoológico!

STUART ¿Qué animales te gusta ver?

PALOMA Los monos son mis favoritos. Son muy chistosos.

STUART A mi, me gustan las jirafas y los elefantes. Son tan grandes.

PALOMA Quiero ver los pájaros también.

STUART Hay mucha variedad de pájaros y aves aquí.

Questions

1. ¿Dónde están Stuart y Paloma?

2. ¿Qué animales le gusta ver a Paloma?

3. ¿Por qué a Paloma le gusta ver esos animales?

4. ¿Qué animales le gusta ver a Stuart?

5. ¿Por qué a Stuart le gusta ver esos animales?

6. ¿El zoológico tiene mucha variedad de pájaros y aves?

Answers: 1. el zoológico 2. los monos 3. Porque son muy chistosos. 4. las jirafas y los elefantes 5. Porque son tan grandes. 6. Sí.

Lessons 93–96

Answer in Spanish.

1. Where do you go to borrow books? _____

2. Where do you go to buy books? _____

3. Where do you get your hair cut? _____

4. Where do you see live animals in enclosed exhibits? _____

Read the conversation and then answer the questions in Spanish.

Buenas noches, soy su mesera. ¿Está lista para pedir?

¿Qué me recomienda?

Los camarones a la parrilla son deliciosos.

Voy a pedir eso.

¿Y qué le gustaría para tomar?

Un agua sin hielo.

5. What does the customer first ask the server? _____

6. What does the customer order to eat? _____

7. How does the server ask the customer what she wants to drink? _____
_____

8. What does the customer order to drink? _____

Translate the following terms from Spanish to English.

9. tenedor _____

10. cuchara _____

11. cuchillo _____

12. cubiertos _____

13. servilleta _____

14. efectivo _____

Correct the bold words in the following sentences.

15. Necesito **levar** y **curtar** mi **caballo**. _____

16. Las **avas** son pájaros. _____

17. Los **manos** están en el zoológico. _____

Reason to Celebrate

172

Happy Birthday!

Key Terms and Phrases

¡Bienvenidos a mi fiesta!	Welcome to my party!
¡Feliz cumpleaños!	Happy birthday!
Voy a cumplir . . . años.	I'm going to turn . . . years old.
el regalo	gift
Voy a abrirlo después del pastel.	I'm going to open it after we eat cake.

Conversation

PALOMA ¡Bienvenidos a mi fiesta!

STUART ¡Feliz cumpleaños! ¿Cuántos años tienes?

PALOMA Voy a cumplir 11 años mañana.

STUART Tengo un regalo para ti.

PALOMA ¡Gracias! Voy a abrirlo después del pastel.

Questions

1. ¿Dónde están Stuart y Paloma?
2. ¿Cómo se dice *Happy birthday* en español?
3. ¿Cuántos años va a cumplir Paloma?
4. ¿Qué tiene Stuart para Paloma?
5. ¿Cuándo va a abrirlo?

Answers: 1. en la fiesta de Paloma 2. feliz cumpleaños 3. 11 4. un regalo 5. después del pastel

> ### NOTES
> *Cumplir* means *to achieve or carry out*, but in the context of birthdays, it means *to turn*.
>
> The happy birthday song in Spanish is the same melody as the English version, and the words are *Cumpleaños feliz, deseamos a ti, cumpleaños a (person's name). Cumpleaños feliz.*
>
> In Mexico, it is common to sing a song called "Las Mañanitas" for one's birthday.

Coming of Age—Turning 15

Key Terms and Phrases

¡Vamos a una quinceañera!	We are going to a birthday celebration for a girl who is turning 15!
¿Es esta tradición sólo para mujeres?	Is it only for women?
¡Qué elegante!	How fancy!
Su vestido es muy hermoso.	Her dress is very beautiful.

Conversation

PALOMA ¡Vamos a una quinceañera!

STUART Sí, estamos celebrando el 15° cumpleaños de nuestra amiga. ¿Es esta tradición solo para mujeres?

PALOMA Sí. ¡Qué elegante la fiesta! Su vestido es muy hermoso.

> **NOTES**
>
> *La quinceañera* is a celebration of a girl's fifteenth birthday and her transition from childhood to adulthood. It involves both a religious ceremony and a party. It is a very important celebration for most Latina girls, and a significant amount of time and money is spent hosting it. Some *quinceañeras* include seven to fourteen girls/women and seven to fourteen boys/men on the "court," which is usually composed of the girl's family and her best friends. The court's duties are to help with planning, to take part in dances, or whatever other help is needed. Food and drinks are an important part of the event, as is the girl's dress. People wear formal attire to a *quinceañera*. The birthday girl's dress can look similar to a wedding dress.

Questions

1. ¿Dónde están Stuart y Paloma?

2. ¿Cuántos años cumple su amiga?

3. ¿Es esta tradición sólo para mujeres?

4. ¿Cómo es su vestido?

Answers: 1. una quinceañera   2. 15   3. Sí.   4. muy hermoso

Happy New Year!

Key Terms and Phrases

¡Feliz año nuevo!	Happy New Year!
la Víspera de Año Nuevo/la Nochevieja	New Year's Eve
Las uvas representan cada mes del año.	The grapes represent each month of the year.
Una uva por mes significa buena suerte.	One grape per month means good luck.
Hay que comer las 12 uvas rápido.	You have to eat the 12 grapes quickly.
¡Que todos tengan mucha suerte el próximo año!	Wishing everybody a lot of luck next year!

Conversation

PACO ¡Feliz año nuevo!

MATEO Me encanta la Víspera de Año Nuevo con familia y amigos.

MARÍA Vamos a comer las 12 uvas pronto.

PALOMA ¿Qué representa cada uva?

STUART Las uvas representan cada mes del año.

PACO Sí, una uva por mes significa buena suerte en el año nuevo.

MATEO Hay que comer las 12 uvas rápido.

MARÍA ¡Que todos tengan mucha suerte el próximo año!

Questions

1. ¿Cómo se dice *Happy New Year* en español?

2. What are two ways to say *New Year's Eve* in Spanish?

3. ¿Qué representa cada uva?

4. ¿Por qué se comen las 12 uvas en la Víspera de Año Nuevo?

5. ¿Hay que comer las 12 uvas rápido?

Answers: 1. ¡Feliz año nuevo!   2. la Víspera de Año Nuevo, la Nochevieja   3. Las uvas representan cada mes del año.   4. Porque una uva por mes significa buena suerte en el año nuevo.   5. Sí.

Lessons 97–99

Read the paragraph and then answer the questions in Spanish.

Es el cumpleaños de Raquel. Ella va a cumplir 15 años manaña y ella está en su gran fiesta. Esta fiesta se llama la quinceañera. Hay muchas personas, y Raquel va a abrir regalos. Su vestido es muy hermoso. Las personas van a comer pastel y celebrar.

1. Whose birthday is it? _____

2. How old will she be tomorrow? _____

3. What's the name of her party? _____

4. What is Raquel going to open? _____

5. What is she wearing that is lovely? _____

6. What are the people going to eat? _____

Translate the following sentences from English to Spanish.

7. Happy New Year! _____

8. Happy birthday! _____

9. It's New Year's Eve. _____

10. One grape per month means good luck. _____

Free at Last!

Key Terms and Phrases

¡Feliz Día de la Independencia!	Happy Independence Day!
celebrar independencia	celebrate independence
ganaron su independencia	won their independence
entre los años	between the years
Había muchas guerras y batallas contra . . .	There were many wars and battles against . . .
Y muchos líderes, pero el más famoso es . . .	And many leaders, but the most famous is . . .
los desfiles	parades
los fuegos artificiales	fireworks

Conversation

PACO En el mes de septiembre muchos países celebran su independencia de España.

MATEO Es verdad. ¿Qué países celebran el 15 de septiembre?

PACO Costa Rica, El Salvador, Guatemala, Honduras y Nicaragua.

MATEO ¿Qué país celebra el 16 de septiembre?

PACO México. ¿Sabe qué países celebran independencia en julio?

MATEO Creo que sí. Argentina, Colombia, Perú y Venezuela ganaron su independencia en julio.

PACO Es verdad. Casi todos los países en América Latina ganaron su independencia entre los años 1810 y 1825.

MATEO Había muchas guerras y batallas contra España.

PACO Sí, y muchos líderes, pero el más famoso es Simón Bolívar.

MATEO En Paraguay decimos "¡Feliz Día de la Independencia!" el 15 de mayo.

PACO En muchos países se celebra con desfiles y fuegos artificiales.

CONTINUED

Questions

1. ¿Cómo se dice *Happy Independence Day* en español?

2. ¿Qué países celebran el 15 de septiembre?

3. ¿Qué país celebra el 16 de septiembre?

4. ¿Entre qué años ganaron la independencia muchos países?

5. ¿Quién es el líder más famoso de la independencia?

6. ¿Cómo se celebra el día de la independencia?

Answers: 1. Feliz Día de la Independencia   2. Costa Rica, El Salvador, Guatemala, Honduras y Nicaragua   3. México   4. 1810 y 1825   5. Simón Bolívar   6. con desfiles y fuegos artificiales

Welcome to My Country!

Key Terms and Phrases

Quiero decirles . . .	I want to tell them . . .
Bienvenidos a este país.	Welcome to this country.
¿Por qué hay tanta gente?	Why are there so many people?
Algunos son turistas.	Some are tourists.
Algunos son inmigrantes.	Some are immigrants.
Algunos están buscando asilo.	Some are seeking asylum.
Algunos son refugiados.	Some are refugees.
La gente emigra para una vida mejor.	People immigrate for a better life.
escaparse de malas condiciones en sus países nativos	to escape bad conditions in their native countries
Exacto, como todos nosotros.	Exactly, like all of us.

Conversation

PACO   Hay muchas personas de otros países aquí.

MATEO   Quiero decirles "¡Bienvenidos a este país!"

STUART   ¿Por qué hay tanta gente?

MAR   Algunos son turistas y algunos son inmigrantes.

PACO   Es verdad. Algunos son refugiados y otros están buscando asilo.

MATEO   Se están escapando de malas condiciones en sus países nativos.

PALOMA   La gente emigra para una vida mejor.

PACO   Exacto, como todos nosotros.

CONTINUED

Questions

1. ¿Cómo se dice *Welcome to this country* en español?

2. ¿Cómo se llaman las personas quien está solo visitando un país?

3. ¿Por qué algunos son refugiados o están buscando asilo?

4. ¿Por qué la gente emigra?

Answers: 1. Bienvenidos a este país.   **2.** turistas   **3.** Porque se están escapando de malas condiciones en sus países nativos.   **4.** Para una vida mejor.

Lessons 100–101

Complete the paragraph with the Spanish terms that make the most sense.

Cada septiembre muchos países (1) _____ su independencia. Casi

todos los países en (2) _____ celebran el 15 de septiembre. México ganó su

(3) _____ de España el 16 de septiembre. Casi todos los países en América

Latina ganaron su independencia (4) _____ los años 1810 y 1825. Había

muchas guerras y batallas contra (5) _____ . Se celebra con desfiles y

(6) _____ artificiales.

Translate the following sentences from English to Spanish.

7. People immigrate for a better life. _____

8. Some are tourists. _____

9. Some are immigrants. _____

10. Some are refugees. _____

11. Some are seeking asylum. _____

12. Welcome to this country! _____

REGULAR VERB CONJUGATIONS

Spanish regular verbs are categorized into three conjugations: those ending in -*ar*, those ending in -*er*, and those ending in -*ir*; for example, *hablar, comer,* and *vivir.*

-ar

yo	hablo
tú	hablas
él, ella, usted	habla
nosotros/nosotras	hablamos
ellos, ellas, ustedes	hablan

-ir

yo	vivo
tú	vives
él, ella, usted	vive
nosotros/nosotras	vivimos
ellos, ellas, ustedes	viven

-er

yo	como
tú	comes
él, ella, usted	come
nosotros/nosotras	comemos
ellos, ellas, ustedes	comen

Notes

In Argentina, Uruguay, and parts of Central America (Costa Rica, El Salvador, and so on), *vos* is used instead of *tú*. Its verb conjugation is similar, but the emphasis is on the last syllable; for example, *Vos hablás, Vos comés,* and *Vos vivís. Vos* is the singular of *vosotros* (*you* plural informal).

In Spain, *vosotros/vosotras* is used instead of *ustedes* to indicate *you* plural informal; for example, *Vosotros habláis, Vosotros coméis,* and *Vosotros vivís.* The stress is on the last syllable of the verb.

COMMON IRREGULAR VERB CONJUGATIONS

Ser (To Be)

yo	soy
tú	eres
él, ella, usted	es
nosotros/nosotras	somos
ellos, ellas, ustedes	son

Notes

- Use *ser* when describing things that are more or less permanent, such as when describing people or things, a person's profession, possessions, relationships, and the time.
- In Spain, *you* plural informal is *Vosotros/Vosotras sois.*
- In Argentina, Uruguay, Costa Rica, and El Salvador, instead of *tú*, use *vos*, and instead of *eres*, use *sos*.

Estar (To Be)

yo	estoy
tú	estás
él, ella, usted	está
nosotros/nosotras	estamos
ellos, ellas, ustedes	están

Notes

- Use *estar* when describing things that are more or less temporary, such as when describing mood and location and using the present progressive (*Ella está hablando = She is talking*).
- In Spain, *you* plural informal is *Vosotros/Vosotras estáis.*

Ir (To Go)

yo	voy
tú	vas
él, ella, usted	va
nosotros/nosotras	vamos
ellos, ellas, ustedes	van

Notes

- In Spain, *you* plural informal is *Vosotros/ Vosotras vais.*

Conocer (To Know)

yo	conozco
tú	conoces
él, ella, usted	conoce
nosotros/nosotras	conocemos
ellos, ellas, ustedes	conocen

Notes

- Use *conocer* to indicate that you know or are familiar with people, places, and things.
- In Spain, *you* plural informal is *Vosotros/ Vosotras conocéis.*

Tener (To Have)

yo	tengo
tú	tienes
él, ella, usted	tiene
nosotros/nosotras	tenemos
ellos, ellas, ustedes	tienen

Notes

- In Spain, *you* plural informal is *Vosotros/ Vosotras tenéis.*

Saber (To Know)

yo	sé
tú	sabes
él, ella, usted	sabe
nosotros/nosotras	sabemos
ellos, ellas, ustedes	saben

Notes

- Use *saber* to indicate that you know facts, information, and how to do something.
- In Spain, *you* plural informal is *Vosotros/ Vosotras sabéis.*

NUMBERS: LOS NÚMEROS

0 cero *[SEH-roh]*

1 uno *[OO-noh]*

2 dos *[DOHS]*

3 tres *[TREHS]*

4 cuatro *[KWA-troh]*

5 cinco *[SEEN-koh]*

6 seis *[SEHees]*

7 siete *[see-EH-teh]*

8 ocho *[OH-choh]*

9 nueve *[noo-EH-veh]*

10 diez *[dee-EHS]*

11 once *[OHN-seh]*

12 doce *[DOH-seh]*

13 trece *[TREH-seh]*

14 catorce *[kah-TOHR-seh]*

15 quince *[KEEN-seh]*

16 dieciseis
[dee-ehs-ee-SEHees]

17 diecisiete
[dee-ehs-ee-see-EH-teh]

18 dieciocho
[dee-ehs-ee-OH-choh]

19 diecinueve
[dee-ehs-ee-noo-EH-veh]

20 veinte *[VEH-een-teh]*

30 treinta *[TREH-een-tah]*

40 cuarenta *[kwah-REHN-tah]*

50 cincuenta *[seen-KWEHN-tah]*

60 sesenta *[seh-SEHN-tah]*

70 setenta *[seh-TEHN-tah]*

80 ochenta *[oh-CHEHN-tah]*

90 noventa *[noh-VEHN-tah]*

For all numbers that are between 20 and 30, 30 and 40, and so on, simply add *y* ["ee"], which means *and*; for example:

33 treinta y tres
[TREH-een-tah ee TREHS]

81 ochenta y uno
[oh-CHEHN-tah ee OO-noh]

Knowing the larger numbers is very useful when talking about currencies in some Spanish-speaking countries.

100 cien *[SEE-ehn]*

200 doscientos
[dohssee-EHN-tohs]

300 trescientos
[trehs-see-EHN-tohs]

400 cuatrocientos
[kwah-troh-see-EHN-tohs]

500 quinientos
[keen-ee-EHN-tohs]

600 seiscientos
[SEHees-see-EHN-tohs]

700 setecientos
[seh-teh-see-EHN-tohs]

800 ochocientos
[oh-choh-see-EHN-tohs]

900 novecientos
[noh-veh-see-EHN-tohs]

1,000 mil *[MEEL]*

PRONOUNS

yo	I
tú	you (singular informal)
él, ella	he, she
usted	you (singular formal)
nosotros, nosotras	we (male/female)
ellos, ellas	they (male/female)
ustedes	you (plural)

Variations

Spain: vosotros, vosotras	you (plural informal, male/female)
Argentina, Uruguay, Costa Rica, and El Salvador: vos	you (singular informal)

ANSWER KEY

Quiz 1: Lessons 1–5

1. Gracias
2. ¿Cómo se escribe?
3. Hola
4. el nombre
5. ¿Cómo se llama?
6. Mucho gusto
7. Igualmente
8. Buenos días
9. Me llamo
10. Te presento
11. el amigo
12. señora
13. señor

Quiz 2: Lessons 6–8

¿Hablan español?	Do you (plural) speak Spanish?
¿De dónde es?	Where are you (singular formal) from?
No hablo español.	I don't speak Spanish.
Escocia	Scotland
Él es de los Estados Unidos.	He's from the United States.
Hablo inglés.	I speak English.
¿De dónde eres?	Where are you (singular informal) from?
Inglaterra	England
¿Cómo se dice?	How do you say?

Quiz 3: Lessons 9–12

1. Paloma es una niña y una hija.
2. Stuart es un niño y un hijo.
3. Daniel es un hombre y un padre.
4. Susana es una mujer y una madre.
5. Claudia es una hermana y una tía.
6. David es un hermano y un tío.
7. Luis es un abuelo.
8. Ana es una abuela.
9. Los niños son primos.
10. La familia tiene mascotas.
11. perro
12. gato
13. pájaro
14. conejo

Quiz 4: Lessons 13–17

1. bajo
2. barato
3. despierto
4. soltero
5. pequeño
6. frío
7. Él está ocupado.
8. Paloma is pretty.
9. Mateo is lucky.
10. viejo
11. sed; hambre
12. blanca; negra.

¿Cuáles colores les gustan?	Which colors do you (plural) like?
Le gusta el azul.	He likes blue.
Le gusta el verde.	She likes green.
Me gusta el rojo.	I like red.
¿Te gusta el amarillo?	Do you (singular informal) like yellow?
El perro es café.	The dog is brown.
No me gusta el morado.	I don't like purple.

Quiz 5: Lessons 18–21

1. Sus
2. tu
3. Su
4. nuestra
5. Mi
6. ciudadano
7. código del país
8. número de teléfono
9. dirección
10. tiene

Quiz 6: Lessons 22–27

1. mañana
2. jueves
3. sábado; domingo
4. mediodía
5. V
6. F
7. F
8. Nos
9. se
10. Me
11. te

Nos levantamos	a las 6:45.
Vamos a la escuela	a las 8:00.
Nos vestimos	a las 7:00.
Desayunamos en casa	a las 7:15.

Quiz 7: Lessons 28–34

1. marzo, abril, or mayo
2. el verano
3. enero
4. diciembre
5. el invierno
6. el otoño
7. un paraguas or una sombrilla
8. el 1 de enero
9. la temporada de lluvias
10. Hace viento.
11. el 15 de marzo
12. el 10 de mayo
13. el 7 de febrero
14. el 1 de agosto or el primer de agosto

Quiz 8: Lessons 35–36

Paco está	enojado.
Stuart y Paco están	aburridos.
Paloma está	emocionada.
Nosotras estamos	listas.

1. triste
2. mal
3. aburrido
4. ¿Qué te pasa?
5. Estoy listo (lista).
6. No te preocupes.
7. Estamos bien.
8. Están tristes.

Quiz 9: Lessons 37–39

1. ¿Qué le pasa? and ¿Dónde le duele?
2. Me gustaría tener (o pedir) una cita.
3. la boca
4. la pasta dental
5. Me alegro.
6. dientes
7. mano
8. garganta
9. pie
10. nariz

las orejas	ears
el pecho	chest
la espalda	back
el corazón	heart
la cabeza	head
el estómago	stomach
el brazo	arm
la pierna	leg

Quiz 10: Lessons 40–45

1. un médico
2. derecho
3. dónde
4. fuera
5. tire
6. El mecánico
7. marque
8. una licencia
9. carro or coche
10. ¡Qué pena! or ¡Qué lástima!
11. manejar; conducir

Quiz 11: Lesson 46–50

1. enseña
2. aprender
3. enfermo; enfermera
4. pedir; mesera
5. tarjetas
6. ladrón; policía
7. incendio; bomberos
8. lapices; plumas; cuadernos
9. la cuenta
10. Ella está herida.
11. Votamos por el senador y el presidente.

Quiz 12: Lessons 51–55

1. están
2. está
3. estás
4. estamos
5. estoy
6. tareas; deberes; trabajos

Están usando sus teléfonos.	They're using their phones.
Estoy duchándome.	I'm taking a shower.
Ella está mirando televisión.	She's watching TV.
Estamos comiendo.	We're eating.

7. usando
8. tampoco
9. Qué
10. nadar; to swim
11. piscina; pool
12. mojado; wet
13. iglesia; church
14. Mis sentidas condolencias or Siento mucho su pérdida.

Quiz 13: Lessons 56–58

1. la cocina
2. el comedor
3. el baño
4. el cuarto
5. la oficina
6. el sótano
7. el jardín
8. Bienvenidos a mi casa.
9. Su casa es muy bonita.
10. Siéntese, por favor.
11. la habitación, el dormitorio, or la recámara
12. How much is the rent?
13. How many bedrooms would you like?
14. Utilities are included.
15. I'd like to rent it.

Quiz 14: Lessons 59–65

1. vamos
2. va
3. van
4. voy
5. vas
6. billete; boleto
7. en carro; en avión; en tren; en taxi; en bus; en barco; a pie

¿Tiene su tarjeta de embarque?	Do you have your boarding pass?
¿Cómo van a viajar?	How are you going to travel?
¿Cuál es el número de puerta para el vuelo?	What's the flight's gate number?
¿Cómo le puedo ayudar?	How may I help you?
¿Dónde está el reclamo de equipaje?	Where is baggage claim?
¿Dónde puedo comprar?	Where can I buy . . . ?

8. Me gustaría alquilar un carro automático por una semana con seguro, por favor.

Quiz 15: Lessons 66–69

1. Slow down.
2. a stop sign
3. the speed limit
4. a one-way street
5. parking
6. How much is the toll?
7. tráfico; traffic
8. semáforo; traffic light
9. playa; beach
10. bloqueador; sunscreen
11. toalla; towel
12. Me gustaría reservar una habitación.
13. con dos camas y un baño privado

Quiz 16: Lessons 70–73

1. el océano
2. la costa
3. las valles
4. los volcanes
5. la selva
6. los desiertos
7. las montañas
8. Have you tried dancing the tango?
9. Have you seen the waterfalls in Argentina?
10. They're on the border.
11. Let's go.
12. One drinks it in Paraguay.
13. Me gusta bailar contigo.
14. El tango viene de Argentina y Uruguay.
15. Me gustan los pasos y la música.

Quiz 17: Lessons 74–77

1. Imperio
2. América Latina
3. llegada
4. capital
5. También
6. parte
7. idioma
8. equator
9. los Andes
10. Sí.
11. V
12. V
13. F; El volcán mas alto del mundo está en Ecuador.
14. F; Venezuela, Colombia, Ecuador, Perú, Bolivia, Argentina y Chile son los países que atraviesan los Andes.

Quiz 18: Lessons 78–79

1. se habla
2. países
3. también
4. antes de
5. siglo
6. Centroamérica; América Central
7. F; Panamá tiene un canal famoso.
8. V
9. F; En Belice se habla más inglés.
10. V
11. F; Hay islas bonitas cerca de Honduras.
12. I haven't been to the countries in Central America.

Quiz 19: Lessons 80–82

Puerto Rico se llama "la isla del encanto".	Puerto Rico is called "the Island of Enchantment."
La isla tiene buen clima todo el año.	The island has good weather all year.
Estoy muy emocionada.	I'm very excited.
Tengo pasaporte americano.	I have an American passport.
No es un estado.	It is not a state.

1. Cuba
2. la República Dominicana
3. Puerto Rico
4. sé
5. Europa
6. Castellano
7. catalán
8. ciudades

Quiz 20: Lessons 83–84

1. bufandas
2. playeras
3. traje de baño
4. sandalias o chanclas
5. guantes
6. bufanda
7. What are we going to buy?
8. I need new clothes for the cold weather.
9. You have clothes for the warm weather.
10. I already have a coat and pants.

Quiz 21: Lessons 85–88

1. pan, maíz, cebollas
2. plátanos, naranjas, pasteles
3. carne, pollo, puerco, pescado
4. lechuga, puerco
5. cuesta
6. un buen
7. ayudar
8. gustan
9. Qué
10. dólares
11. patatas
12. verduras

Quiz 22: Lessons 89–92

Está hecho a mano.	It's made by hand.
¿Cuál es su mejor precio?	What's your best price?
Cobra demasiado.	You charge too much.
Le doy cinco.	I'll give you five.

1. el cine
2. trata
3. empieza
4. termina
5. entradas
6. pelota; ball
7. deporte; sport
8. equipo; team
9. béisbol; baseball
10. juego; game
11. Le encanta jugar fútbol.
12. El baloncesto es su deporte favorito.
13. Ellos van a esquiar.
14. Me gusta patinar.

Quiz 23: Lessons 93–96

1. la biblioteca
2. la librería
3. el salón de belleza
4. el zoológico
5. ¿Qué me recomienda?
6. los camarones a la parrilla
7. ¿Y qué le gustaría para tomar?
8. un agua sin hielo
9. fork
10. spoon
11. knife
12. utensils
13. napkin
14. cash
15. lavar; cortar; cabello
16. aves
17. monos

Quiz 24: Lessons 97–99

1. Raquel
2. 15
3. la quinceañera
4. regalos
5. un vestido
6. pastel
7. ¡Feliz año nuevo!
8. ¡Feliz cumpleaños!
9. Es la Víspera de Año Nuevo.
10. Una uva por mes significa buena suerte.

Quiz 25: Lessons 100–101

1. celebran
2. Centroamérica
3. independencia
4. entre
5. España
6. fuegos
7. La gente emigra para una vida mejor.
8. Algunos son turistas.
9. Algunos son inmigrantes.
10. Algunos son refugiados.
11. Algunos están buscando asilo.
12. ¡Bienvenidos a este país!

BASIC VOCABULARY

The gender of Spanish nouns is indicated by an article, either *el* (masculine) or *la* (feminine). In cases where a noun can be either masculine or feminine, it is first written in the masculine form and then the feminine in parentheses; for example, **niño, el (la niña)**. To make the singular noun a plural noun, change *el* to *los* and *la* to *las* and (usually) add *s* or *es* to the end of the noun.

A	to	**APARTAMENTO, EL**	apartment
ABRIGO, EL	coat	**ARENA, LA**	sand
ABRIL	April	**AUTOBÚS, EL**	bus
ABUELO, EL (LA ABUELA)	grandfather/grandmother	**AVIÓN, EL**	airplane
ACCIDENTE, EL	accident	**BALONCESTO, EL**	basketball
ACEITE, EL	oil	**BAÑO, EL**	bathroom
ACONDICIONADOR, EL	conditioner	**BARCO, EL**	boat
AEROPUERTO, EL	airport	**BÉISBOL, EL**	baseball
AGENTE, EL (LA AGENTE)	agent	**BIBLIOTECA, LA**	library
AGOSTO	August	**BILLETE, EL**	ticket
AGUA, EL	water	**BLOQUE, EL**	city block
ALMUERZO, EL	lunch	**BLOQUEADOR, EL**	sunscreen
ALQUILER, EL	the rent	**BOCA, LA**	mouth
AMÉRICA CENTRAL	Central America	**BOLETO, EL**	ticket
AMÉRICA LATINA	Latin America	**BOMBERO, EL (LA BOMBERA)**	firefighter
AMIGO, EL (LA AMIGA)	friend	**BOMBILLA, LA**	straw (for drinking)
ANFITRIÓN, EL (LA ANFITRIONA)	host/hostess	**BOSQUE, EL**	forest
AÑO, EL	year	**BRAZO, EL**	arm
		BUFANDA, LA	scarf

CABELLO, EL	hair (as in "head of hair")
CABEZA, LA	head
CABINA DE PEAJE, LA	tollbooth
CAJERO, EL	cashier
CALLE, LA	street
CALOR, EL	heat
CAMA, LA	bed
CAMERONES, LOS	shrimp
CAMISETA, LA	shirt
CANAL, EL	canal
CAPITAL, LA	capital
CARIBE, EL	the Caribbean
CARIES, LAS	cavities
CARNE, EL	meat
CARNICERÍA, LA	butcher shop
CARNICERO, EL (LA CARNICERA)	butcher
CARRO, EL	car
CASA, LA	home/house
CASCADA, LA	waterfall
CATARATA, LA	waterfall
CEBOLLA, LA	onion
CENTROAMÉRICA	Central America
CEPILLO DE DIENTES, EL	toothbrush
CHAMPÚ, EL	shampoo
CIRUGÍA, LA	surgery
CITA, LA	appointment
CIUDAD, LA	city
CIUDADANO, EL (LA CIUDADANA)	citizen
CLASE, LA	class
CLIMA, EL	weather
COCHE, EL	car
COCINA, LA	kitchen
CÓDIGO DEL PAÍS, EL	country code
COLOR, EL	color
COLLAR, EL	necklace
COMEDOR, EL	dining room
CONDOLENCIAS, LAS	condolences
CONEJO, EL	rabbit
CORAZÓN, EL	heart
CORDILLERA, LA	mountain range
COSTA, LA	coast
CUADERNO, EL	notebook
CUADRA, LA	city block
CUARTO, EL	bedroom
CUBIERTOS, LOS	eating utensils
CUCHARA, LA	spoon
CUCHILLO, EL	knife
CUENTA, LA	bill (to pay)

CUMPLEAÑOS, EL	birthday
DEBERES, LOS	assignments/tasks/errands
DENTISTA, EL (LA DENTISTA)	dentist
DEPARTAMENTO, EL	apartment
DEPORTE, EL	sport
DEPÓSITO, EL	deposit
DERECHA, LA	right (direction)
DESAYUNO, EL	breakfast
DESFILE, EL	parade
DESIERTO, EL	desert
DÍA, EL	day
DIARREA, LA	diarrhea
DICIEMBRE	December
DIENTE, EL	tooth
DIPUTADO, EL (LA DIPUTADA)	congressman/congresswoman
DIRECCIÓN, LA	address
DOCTOR, EL (LA DOCTORA)	doctor
DÓLAR, EL	dollar
DOMINGO, EL	Sunday
DORMITORIO, EL	bedroom
ECUADOR, EL	equator
EFECTIVO, EL	cash
ELEFANTE, EL	elephant
ENERO	January
ENFERMERO, EL (LA ENFERMERA)	nurse
ENTRADA, LA	ticket
EQUIPAJE, EL	luggage
EQUIPAJE DE MANO, EL	carry-on luggage
EQUIPO, EL	team
ESCUELA, LA	school
ESPALDA, LA	back (body part)
ESPAÑA	Spain
ESPAÑOL, EL	Spanish
ESPOSO, EL (LA ESPOSA)	husband/wife
ESQUÍS, LOS	skis
ESTACIÓN, LA	station or season
ESTACIONAMIENTO, EL	parking
ESTADO, EL	state (geographical region)
ESTADOS UNIDOS, LOS	United States
ESTILISTA, EL/LA	hairstylist
ESTÓMAGO, EL	stomach
ESTUDIANTE, EL (LA ESTUDIANTE)	student
FAMILIA, LA	family
FEBRERO	February
FECHA, LA	date (on the calendar)
FIESTA, LA	party
FIN DE SEMANA, EL	weekend
FRENOS, LOS	brakes

FRESA, LA	strawberry	**HOTEL, EL**	hotel
FRÍO, EL	cold	**HOY**	today
FRONTERA, LA	border	**HURACÁN, EL**	hurricane
FRUTA, LA	fruit	**IDIOMA, EL**	language
FUEGO, EL	fire	**IGLESIA, LA**	church
FUNERAL, EL	funeral	**IMPERIO, EL**	empire
FÚTBOL, EL	soccer	**INCENDIO, EL**	fire (large)
FÚTBOL AMERICANO, EL	football	**INDEPENDENCIA, LA**	independence
GARGANTA, LA	throat	**INGLÉS, EL**	English
GATO, EL	cat	**INMIGRANTE, EL (LA INMIGRANTE)**	immigrant
GENTE, LA	people	**INUNDACIÓN, LA**	flood
GLACIAR, EL	glacier	**INVIERNO, EL**	winter
GOBIERNO, EL	government	**ISLA, LA**	island
GRACIAS	thank you	**IZQUIERDA, LA**	left (direction)
GUANTE, EL	glove	**JARDÍN, EL**	yard
GUERRA, LA	war	**JIRAFA, LA**	giraffe
HABITACIÓN, LA	bedroom	**JUEGO, EL**	game
HAMBRE, EL	hunger	**JUEVES, EL**	Thursday
HERMANO, EL (LA HERMANA)	brother/sister	**JUGO, EL**	juice
HIELO, EL	ice	**JULIO**	July
HIJO, EL (LA HIJA)	son/daughter	**JUNIO**	June
HOLA	hello	**KILOMETRAJE, EL**	mileage
HOMBRE, EL	man	**LADRÓN, EL (LA LADRONA)**	thief
HORARIO, EL	schedule	**LAGO, EL**	lake

LÁPIZ, EL	pencil
LECHUGA, LA	lettuce
LECTURA, LA	reading (school subject)
LEY, LA	law
LIBRERÍA, LA	bookstore
LIBRO, EL	book
LÍMITE DE VELOCIDAD, EL	speed limit
LUNES, EL	Monday
LLANTA, LA	tire
LLAVE, LA	key
LLEGADA, LA	arrival
LLUVIA, LA	rain
MADRE, LA	mother
MAESTRO, EL (LA MAESTRA)	teacher
MAÍZ, EL	corn
MALETA, LA	suitcase
MANO, LA	hand
MANZANA, LA	apple or city block
MAÑANA	tomorrow
MAPA, EL	map
MARISCOS, LOS	seafood
MARTES, EL	Tuesday
MARZO	March
MASCOTA, LA	pet
MAYO	May

MECÁNICO, EL (LA MECÁNICA)	mechanic
MEDICINA, LA	medicine
MÉDICO, EL (LA MÉDICA)	doctor
MEDIODÍA, EL	noon
MERCADO, EL	market
MES, EL	month
MESERO, EL (LA MESERA)	server
MIÉRCOLES, EL	Wednesday
MONO, EL	monkey
MONTAÑA, LA	mountain
MOTOR, EL	engine
MUCHO	a lot
MUERTE, LA	death
MUJER, LA	woman
MULTA, LA	fine
MUNDO, EL	world
MÚSICA, LA	music
NARANJA, LA	orange
NARIZ, LA	nose
NIÑO, EL (LA NIÑA)	boy/girl
NOMBRE, EL	name
NOVIEMBRE	November
NÚMERO, EL	number
NÚMERO DE PUERTA, EL	gate (at an airport)

NÚMERO DE TELÉFONO, EL	phone number
OCÉANO, EL	ocean
OCTUBRE	October
OFICINA, LA	office
OJO, EL	eye
OLA, LA	wave
OREJA, LA	ear
OTOÑO, EL	autumn/fall
PADRE, EL	father (parent)
PAÍS, EL	country
PÁJARO, EL	bird
PALABRA, LA	word
PAN, EL	bread
PANADERÍA, LA	bakery
PANADERO, EL (LA PANADERA)	baker
PANTALONES, LOS	pants
PANTALONES CORTOS, LOS	shorts
PAPA, LA	potato
PAPEL, EL	paper
PAPEL HIGIÉNICO, EL	toilet paper
PARADA, LA	stop (for travel)
PARAGUAS, EL	umbrella
PARAMÉDICO, EL (LA PARAMÉDICA)	paramedic
PASAPORTE, EL	passport
PASE DE ABORDAR, EL	boarding pass
PASEO, EL	a walk
PASO, EL	step
PASTA DENTAL, LA	toothpaste
PASTEL, EL	cake
PATATA, LA	potato
PATINES, LOS	skates
PATIO, EL	patio
PAZ, LA	peace
PEAJE, EL	toll/tollbooth
PECHO, EL	chest
PELÍCULA, LA	movie
PELOTA, LA	ball
PÉRDIDA, LA	loss
PERSONA, LA	person
PERRO, EL	dog
PESCADO, EL	fish (to eat)
PIE, EL	foot
PIERNA, LA	leg
PIRÁMIDE, LA	pyramid
PISCINA, LA	pool
PISO, EL	floor
PLACAS, LAS	license plates
PLÁTANO, EL	banana/plantain
PLAYA, LA	beach

PLUMA, LA	pen
POCO	a little
POLICÍA, LA	police
POLLO, EL	chicken
PRECIO, EL	price
PRESIDENTE, EL (LA PRESIDENTA)	president
PRIMAVERA, LA	spring
PRIMO, EL (LA PRIMA)	cousin
PROBLEMA, EL	problem
PUERCO, EL	pork
PUNTAS, LAS	ends (of hair)
RAQUETA, LA	racket
RECÁMARA, LA	bedroom
RECLAMO DE EQUIPAJE, EL	baggage claim
REFUGIADO, EL (LA REFUGIADA)	refugee
REGALO, EL	gift
RENTA, LA	rent
RESTAURANTE, EL	restaurant
ROPA, LA	clothes
RUIDO, EL	sound
RUINAS, LAS	ruins
SÁBADO, EL	Saturday
SALA, LA	room (in a house or building)
SALA DE ESTAR, LA	living room

SALÓN, EL	living room
SALÓN DE BELLEZA, EL	beauty salon/hair salon
SALUD, LA	health
SALVAVIDAS, EL (LA SALVAVIDAS)	lifeguard
SANDALIA, LA	sandal
SED, EL	thirst
SEGURO, EL	insurance
SELVA, LA	jungle
SEMÁFORO, EL	traffic light
SEMANA, LA	week
SENADOR, EL (LA SENADORA)	senator
SEÑAL, LA	signal
SEÑAL DE ALTO, LA	stop sign
SEÑOR/SEÑORA	Mr./Ms.
SEPTIEMBRE	September
SERVICIO, EL	service
SERVICIOS, LOS	bathroom
SERVILLETA, LA	napkin
SIGLO, EL	century
SOMBRILLA, LA	umbrella
SOPA, LA	soup
SÓTANO, EL	basement
SUDAMÉRICA	South America
SUERTE, EL	luck

TARDE, LA	afternoon	**TURISTA, EL (LA TURISTA)**	tourist
TAREA, LA	assignment	**UVA, LA**	grape
TARJETA, LA	card	**VALLE, EL**	valley
TARJETA DE CRÉDITO, LA	credit card	**VECINO, EL (LA VECINA)**	neighbor
TAXI, EL	taxi	**VEGETAL, EL**	vegetable
TAXISTA, EL (LA TAXISTA)	taxi driver	**VELOCIDAD, LA**	speed
TELÉFONO, EL	telephone	**VENDEDOR, EL (LA VENDADORA)**	
TELEVISIÓN, LA	television		vendor
TEMPORADA, LA	season	**VERANO, EL**	summer
TENEDOR, EL	fork	**VERDAD, LA**	truth
TENIS, EL	tennis	**VERDURA, LA**	vegetable
TERREMOTO, EL	earthquake	**VESTIDO, EL**	dress
TERRITORIO, EL	territory	**VÍA, LA**	way
TÍO, EL (LA TÍA)	uncle/aunt	**VIAJE, EL**	trip
TIPO, EL	type	**VIDA, LA**	life
TOALLA, LA	towel	**VIERNES, EL**	Friday
TRABAJO, EL	work	**VOLCÁN, EL**	volcano
TRÁFICO, EL	traffic	**VUELO, EL**	flight
TRAJE DE BAÑO, EL	swimsuit	**ZANAHORIA, LA**	carrot
TREN, EL	train	**ZONA, LA**	area
		ZOOLÓGICO, EL	zoo

INDEX

ACKNOWLEDGMENTS

I wish to thank the following friends whose knowledge of the Spanish language and Latin cultures contributed greatly to this book: Veronica Fierro, Raquel Talavera, Roberto Tudor, Emily Kopa, Juan Antonio Ayala, Laura Rodríguez, Silvia Cotacachi, Miguel González-Abellás, and Anna Woods. I'd also like to thank my husband, Matt, and my children, Stuart and Paloma, for their loving support. Saben que mi amor es infinito.

ABOUT THE AUTHOR

Melanie Stuart-Campbell has been an educator of world languages for more than twenty-five years. She loves to travel and is a passionate advocate for bilingualism and world language education, especially *español*. Melanie is the author of *Alba, the South American Street Dog* and resides in Kansas with her husband and two children.

CPSIA information can be obtained
at www.ICGtesting.com
Printed in the USA
BVHW052321151019
561167BV00002B/2